A Daily Prayer, Short and Sweet

Real Conversations with God

W.G. (BILL) HENDERSON JR.

© 2021
Published in the United States by Nurturing Faith, Macon, GA.
Nurturing Faith is a book imprint of Good Faith Media (goodfaithmedia.org).
Library of Congress Cataloging-in-Publication Data is available.

ISBN: 978-1-63528-145-3

All rights reserved. Printed in the United States of America.

All scripture citations are from the New International Version (NIV)
unless otherwise indicated.

Illustrations by Margaret L. Mullis

"Simple, warm, and profound! Each prayer in Bill Henderson's book allows me to begin the day knowing that God's love is real and present in this moment. They are tangible prayers written from real-life experience. Bill captures the life-giving message of the gospel and dispenses it in a daily format that speaks to your soul. His daily prayer allows me to carry that blessing into my day and all of the relationships in my life. They are a balm for the soul, especially in these uncertain, stressful times!"

—*Mary Katherine Robinson. Presbyterian Minister*

"Every day I receive a fresh, earthy prayer that helps me wrestle with the stuff of life—good and bad, delightful and depressing, hopeful and hurtful. Now here they are, collected in one place, ready to use at a moment's notice. Who does not need such help when it's time to pray?"

—*Dwight A. Moody, Host*
www.themeetinghouse.net

"Paul the Apostle wrote, 'Pray without ceasing.' To some this is a monumental task: What do I pray? Bill Henderson's prayers are conversations with God and a help on our journey with Jesus. His prayers are intimate, relational, and relevant and provide the reader with an opportunity to escape again to that place of prayer with the Lord."

—*Dave Gittings, Chaplain*
Virginia Tech Football Team

"I eagerly await Bill Henderson's "Daily Prayers" each morning as a part of my quiet time. These prayers/conversations with God give a fresh, personal focus on faith. What a blessing!"

—*Bill Walker, Former Principal*
Asheville (N.C.) School for Developmentally Disabled

"Bill's prayers meet my needs each day, reflecting the presence of God in circumstances major and minor. Praying with him begins in the physicality of life as well as interacting within God's presence. What a good way to begin a day … or maybe even close it."

—*Gail Coulter, Coordinator,*
Western North Carolina Baptist Fellowship

"I recommend Dr. Henderson's book on prayer. As many of us have come to know, the most vital of all conversations is with our God. It's our source of power and our purpose in the daily living of our days."

—*Buddy Corbin, Chaplain*
Mission Hospital, Asheville, North Carolina

"Henderson's prayers are heartfelt, thought-provoking, and down to earth. You will be blessed by them."

—*Anne Ownbey, Author, Liturgist*

CONTENTS

September
1

October
11

November
21

December
33

January
43

February
55

March
65

April
75

May
85

June
97

July
107

August
119

PREFACE

I have known all my life about prayer. Like breathing in and breathing out, it is just a natural part of moment-by-moment living—every hour, every day. I can remember my mother praying over me at the crib. I can feel her face next to mine, and I knew she was talking to God about me. It was a while before I heard the words, but I remember them like yesterday.

My father prayed for me at the dinner table—long, eloquent, and sincere talks with God, often reminding God of what had been promised, not demanding, just celebrating the unshakeable foundation that had been laid through the generations. Then he prayed at church where prayers are supposed to be spoken—also long, elegant, and sincere while breathing deeply like he was reaching deep into his own soul, the archives of generations of prayers, hurts, cries, along with joys.

My father-in-law prays and admonishes us to pray about everything. He has emblazoned on my mind one well-worn phrase when I have shared my personal struggles or trying times. He has said it often: "Trust your prayers!" Since he talks so much about prayer, I asked him when and how and in what ways he prays. I expected an elaborate scheme of times and means. He rambled around, and I cannot tell you any answers he really offered. My prayers are like that, too. That is part of the motivation for these daily writings: to shape them, sharpen them, and be specific while speaking honestly through love and unbelievably devoted humility.

My folks prayed because they needed a "bulwark never failing." Both of my parents came from good, sweet homes, but had just enough natural difficulties to make a child shiver with uncertainty and learn at church to pray. That's where they learned about prayer. But in their breathing in and breathing out, they learned about the sighs too deep for words—those groanings for which the scriptures say the Spirit finds words.

Then I learned to pray, and as a child it was so natural, so personal, so easy. Until, I must confess, I found it awkward at times as I grew up, even silly to have to put words up in the air for the God who already knew my thoughts, my motives, my heart, my deceit but mostly my genuine desire to please God.

But praying made me reach higher and made me be articulate about feelings that needed expression, thoughts that needed reshaping into higher thoughts, and ultimately random heart firings that needed sensible shaping into life-affirming connections and then real commitments.

So that is where all my real conversations with God are going, headed straight for commitments that I believe and cannot avoid doing something about. In attempting to explain this daily prayer experience with a neighbor who protested that he had, indeed, been reading them daily, I wondered what he did with all this heart-rambling nakedness before God. He said, "Well, these aren't really prayers. They are more like devotionals—no, like blogs with God!" I gulped, then chuckled, then grimaced at the thought.

Here is my final explanation. Like my mother's prayers so early in my life, prayer is my constant thought with God and constant reflection with the one who is said to be always with us, waking, sleeping. I have only sporadically held specific devotional hours or quiet time or regular prayer times. This is just not my style, my discipline. I am at it all the time. So, the words you'll read in the following pages capture only moments with my constant real conversations with God. I pray that these words may stimulate for you reinvigorated conversations with the God who hears and—by grace—answers.

AUTHOR'S NOTE

This book of prayers begins in September right when I began them. I hope that does not confuse you! A typical sequence might be expected on the usual annual calendar starting from January, yet still those pesky fifth weeks come along in their own time. Proper scheduling for devotional reading has eluded me. My excuses are as follows.

These prayers began as the outgrowth of real experience, while caring for an element of homebound members whom I could not see as often as the contact they needed. I greatly revered these whose lives had been living and serving examples among their own church family, whose new retirement residence had isolated them from their church friends. As I visited them, they continually asked for more contact: "Please come visit me more often!" My anxiety was growing in proportion to my love and admiration for these special, aging saints.

"Aha! I can send you a daily contact, a word for reflection. How about a prayer?" Thus, these "contacts" were born. Not long into this experiment, I heard many requests that I might publish and make them available to others. These special folks imagined sharing my daily prayers with their families and closest friends. The email list began to grow.

I learned how important simple contact could be, but much more I saw how the sharing of an open prayer to the Lord opened the door that many people are too humble, too respectful, or too unskilled to open for themselves. These prayers explored avenues that were apparently on the minds and hearts of others, but were never thought to warrant being aired before our Almighty Creator. Are they? Are these too open, too raw to preserve the dignity, the wealth of a relationship with a loving yet mighty Creator? Only time will tell.

If you have the time, you, too, may sense a freedom never allowed before in the context of an open relationship of communication called prayer. If so, may the words of your mouths and the meditations of my heart alongside of yours be acceptable, O Lord, the strength of my life and my prayers and the redeemer of all I attempt. Read on… and pray along with me!

***

These prayers are scheduled according to the seasons in which they were written, from September 2019 through August 2020, and based on those months having five Sundays. Readers may alter the schedule as necessary.

september

WEEK 1

Monday

O Lord,
Because faith seems to be the weakest tool in the toolbox, and because we tend to dress up real faith in God in many disguises as if to hide it from those who might not understand, we become like Joseph of Arimathea or Nicodemus who were "secret followers" of Christ. Embolden our faith and our expressions of it today, O God, and may our honest confessions of love to you give strength to those who are struggling to make their lives count for something. Help us to do good things without shame or embarrassment and apology, that we may add credibility to your name.
Amen

Tuesday

O Lord,
Bring our straggling thoughts and vagrant affections to a focus today, so that we not only find you but also find joy in your presence. You alone satisfy us completely, because we have learned that in all things you work for good with those who love you and know the calling of your purpose. Thank you for calling us.
Amen

Wednesday

O Lord,
I saw the gardened deck of a friend—the lovely growth, so diverse, colorful, and proud. My life is a big pot of growing things, all from seeds planted through the years by passing gardeners and life experiences. Prune back the stalks that threaten to overtake the others, those hardened opinions that I have allowed to take more than their share of the room in my pot, those that feed my opinion of myself and give me the stiffening pride that you see right through and that you hate. Help me to know the feathered feet of butterflies again, those that can taste the sweetness of my life and find it nourishing, the sweet mercy I can offer because it is what you have given me. My big pot is crowded with weeds of this world and needs your gardening touch.
Amen

Thursday

O Lord,
God of love, Father who reaches for the fallen, I stand before you this morning bearing the record of my life. It is stained with false aspiration and brokenness. I am asking again for your patience, that you not turn your face from my stubbornness and pride. As the Psalmist prayed, I plead: "Cast me not from thy presence. Take not thy Holy Spirit from me." You are the shepherd of my soul, and I am just a wayward sheep, cut and bruised and bleeding from briars and unyielding soil. Let your shepherd's rod tap me back to the trail of life. Let your staff pull

me from the deep places, back to the paths of understanding. The way is dark at times, and I cannot find the way. Lead me Lord.
Amen

Friday

O Lord,
Sometimes I get hungry, but today I saw the hungry standing in line at a soup kitchen. Their forlorn faces told of their desperation. I don't know desperation. There but for the grace of God go I. But my soul gets hungry. You make me hungry for grace and more grace, for there is no shortage there. The servers in the line today were happily pouring out the spoonfuls, laughing cheerfully, splashing and loading up the plentiful supply, and I saw food for the hungry bellies, and I saw grace for the hungry souls. What a joyful bunch your servants were, satisfying the hungry! Lord, I want to be in that number, when the saints dish up that love.
Amen

Saturday

O Lord,
She must have been one of your servants, but I didn't have the chance to find out. "I am so thankful," she said, and she was a nurse, telling me that her father had lived ten years more after a heart trouble diagnosis that gave him months to live. Then he had a heart and lung transplant, giving him those ten years, a new heart! Imagine! His life span was over. He had been given the last rites, but it wasn't to be. She said he lived transformed in more than his organs but in his heart of hearts, so to speak. He went from grumbly hateful to humbly grateful in one afternoon with a new chance to live among the people he loved and the home he shared and the life he had built. It changed him! All I could hear was the joy in heaven that must have filled the air. One man, one heart: Isn't that the plan, one at a time?
Amen

Sunday

O Lord,
We are admonished to praise you for your wonderful deeds, and I have learned from my childhood the list, the long list, starting with creation right down to the glorious resurrection of Jesus. But when I found you for myself, when I needed you and found you for me, it was an experience like no other, an awakening to the reality, the truth of all I had always heard about but left in the book. Was that when I stopped my silly rushing after adventure long enough for you to break through to my heart? Or was that the natural putting aside of childish things and I began to see more clearly the presence and power of your love? No matter, the truth of experience with you, O Lord, is greater than all the books can hold, and I praise you in it!
Amen

WEEK 2

Monday

O Lord,

As I sit here listening to the stories of World War II, it is hard to comprehend the scale of the whole world engaged in a fight to the death—all the nations, all the leaders and the peoples. How much hatred and distrust and malice have to grow and spread to engage all of us into such an agreement to suit up and go to kill or be killed? Your ultimate aim for peace on earth and goodwill to all and the message of loving one another as we have been loved, giving as we have been given, equality and justice for all … When does it go silent for this other insidious demand to lay claim to our minds and hearts as the most important thing in the universe? God help us know, love, and reflect your will again.
Amen

Tuesday

O Lord,

My friend Jim dropped off some fresh peaches. "They're from Chilton County, Alabama. Tell your Mama." Last week he brought flags and set them out across the yard for the remembrance of the "war to end all wars." The week before, he dropped off donuts; another week it was homemade brownies; and he just keeps on coming! That is the remarkable part of his gifts: it is himself. He just keeps on coming, reminding these folks that they aren't forgotten. They bring healing! Old wounds disappear like the threat of aging and being forgotten. He is like you, Lord. He keeps on coming, the word becomes flesh, and is always full.
Amen

Wednesday

O Lord,

I sit on the back porch in Georgia and watch the tall trees swaying, reaching, fighting for their stretch of sunlight. They must have it to grow; competing, reaching upward in the forest—hardwoods, evergreens. The huge pines and oaks are staggering. The lone tree with all its claims on the sunlight of its field grows wide and full, not needing to compete for the sunlight it needs. We all are different like that, each with our own mark in our world, reaching for the light, the same sunlight that makes us grow tall and strong and sturdy; your holy light, shining in our lives, illumining our minds, fulfilling our hopes and satisfying our needs. You, Lord: we all need you, Lord!
Amen

Thursday

O Lord,

I love good people, just really good down-to-the-core people. What you see is what you get—not damaged goods or fragile frailties—just good, solid people; people you can depend on;

people who can give you their word without fear and mean it. You know they will do what they said and be what they said they are. Fear has damaged so many. Dysfunctional families have damaged their children. And now the floating ideologies, the wild tales that are filling the airwaves or jamming the social media, ones that are radicalizing some vulnerable ones among us: these are the new ways of twisting and terrorizing us all. I long for the good people. Where are they? Here's one, if you will help me do my best. I'm in this with you, Lord.
Amen

Friday

O Lord,
Mr. Mac used to faithfully come to worship, and we didn't know if he believed—such a self-made man was he. But he would tell me, "I don't know how it works, but it does, somehow." He made so much of his life and his vision, leading in so many areas, loving his wife faithfully, building and blessing his family—things he could only do with your strength, I'm sure! I could see your hands guiding this courageous, life-loving man with every deliberate step he took. Then you took him, at age 99. I saw your face in his, even the occasional doubts, because these never deterred his determination. I want to be that kind of blessing. And to think: it didn't come with a whole lot of right doctrine, just faithfulness.
Amen

Saturday

O Lord,
I want to prepare for worship for tomorrow, really work at clearing my mind and getting my heart ready for receiving some refreshing time in your presence, Lord. Prayer, right? Being quiet or still, right? Reading something that opens me up to your Spirit, scripture, right? Or maybe simply opening my eyes wider than before to all the wonders of your handiwork. There is so much to see, but there are wonders of your love everywhere, too: little things and big, the unseen and the overlooked, the spoken and unspoken. I am getting ready. Or am I already worshipping?
Amen

Sunday

O Lord,
A lovely neighbor has the loveliest pots full of overflowing white geraniums, spilling over, attracting all of us to comment and ask her secrets. She offers them freely: "I pick off the dead and yellowing parts daily. It's easy!" I reflected on our worship, too often lifeless, generically bland, or missing the mark. What courage it takes to point out those ugly thoughts, attitudes, habits, or choices. Worship dare not evasively skip self-scrutiny that removes the dead parts! Make us brave enough, honest and courageous enough to say, "Woe is me, for I am unclean and live among an unclean people!" Make us lovely again.
Amen

WEEK 3

Monday

O Lord,
I love the mountains, I love the rolling hills, I love the flowers and all the daffodils, I love the fireside when all the lights are low. And I hear your words to me: "Except ye enter as a little child, you shall not enter the kingdom of God." And gladly, simply, I come. Struggling to be in charge, I come anyway. Fearful of letting go, I come. Uncertain of a future where you alone are leading, I still come. I am coming, slowly, reluctantly sometimes, but humbly I step out of my little boat into your stormy sea, with you. I come.
Amen

Tuesday

O Lord,
I was feeling pretty good and warm-hearted, and I stopped to say, "Thank you." Then I got a lecture on what everyone else ought to be doing and how ungrateful and how bad things are today. She was just unhappy, and I stood there and took my medicine. The longer I stood, the feelings of warmth and good-heartedness came quietly back into my soul. So I stood, and I listened, and I watched her carefully with genuine interest. She seemed all alone, uncared for, a sheep without a shepherd. I knew again how you felt when you looked out over your ungrateful hometown with pity and sorrow and then with tears. And then I thanked her again for what she was doing, and I saw a faint light coming back into her face. She smiled and thanked me as I turned to leave. That's how it works, right Lord?
Amen

Wednesday

O Lord,
The sad news of a fellow minister taking her own life this week has taken my breath away. None of us knows what is happening inside the mind and heart of another person unless they dare to tell us, and few really dare. Forgive us, Lord, for our busy, self-absorbed rush that denies another the chance to trust and dare. Listening would be such a tender and meaningful gift to another person close to ourselves. We have many reassurances of her inner battles being over now and her darkness turning to light in your arms and your presence. Nothing can separate us from that powerful and persistent love of yours in Christ Jesus our Lord. How sad I am that she lost her battle, that we did, too, and then mostly that you did, Lord, knowing how you loved her. Give her now that desperate rest she sought, I pray.
Amen

Thursday

O Lord,

Time is of the essence, time is short, and time is fleeting. Some would say just eat dessert first, while others would say do all the good you can while you can, because you will not pass this way again. Some easily say time is in your hands; others say no one knows where the time goes. It is certain that I should make the most of my time, for when my time is up, there is no good I can do from the grave. As your child, I have your promise that time is eternal, that life has an everlasting dimension. And rather than sit back and watch it go by, I will invest my time wisely and make the most of my time, with your guiding light, as time goes by quickly.
Amen

Friday

O Lord,

Autumn has arrived. I can feel the brisk air as a welcome break from the heat, and I know you are changing seasons to give the earth its needed relief. The autumn leaves drift by my window; the red and gold signal the change that I love. Your artistry is a changing palette of colors setting the pace for old winter's song. Now autumn can help me understand the necessary deadness about life, the time when changes are necessary, when what has been brilliant must go to make room for the new colors and songs of life, and all of it in your lifegiving cycle of all living things. Here it is, your gift to be fully alive, not just merely comfortable. Help me now, Lord, to shed the old and embrace the new, trusting you all the way.
Amen

Saturday

O Lord,

I want to prepare for tomorrow's worship; to get ready mind, body, and soul. Getting ready is what we have believed in, talked about, begged for from church people coming to worship. Shall I spend extra time in prayer, reading scripture, thinking spiritual thoughts, planning what to do? The Psalmist recalls those mountaintop experiences, lifting his eyes to the hills, the places where you, Lord, had spoken to him, encouraging and strengthening him. I also have had many treasured moments, close to you, knowing your presence and your help. How could I forget? I, too, "will lift up mine eyes" and remember your faithfulness in rare moments when I most needed it. You are indeed my strength and my redeemer.
Amen

Sunday

O Lord,

Let our joy in your service run deep this morning, as we find ourselves partners with others in the same sorrows, the same laughter, the same adversity, and the same prosperity. May we catch a glimpse of your view of our lives, so that we may know that life's pluses and minuses turn out to be a magnificent plus because your greatness has filled every lack and transfigured every blessing.
Amen

WEEK 4

Monday
O Lord,
We thank you for morning light and evening peace, for in the night you restored our spirit's strength and in this day you will lead us into more life. From the past so much has come to bless us, and now the future lifts our eyes in hopefulness. Make the beauty around excite us, the work discipline us, saints encourage us, sinners humble us, and love redeem us.
Amen

Tuesday
O Lord,
So often we have asked that mercy fall on us like showers of rain, plentifully. Today we ask that we could retreat into the secret places within us and find you rising there like a spring, fresh and renewing us. Be close at hand, for we confess that you are the only fountain of life, an overflowing spirit within us.
Amen

Wednesday
O Lord,
Lead me Lord, lead me in thy righteousness. I pray as another prayed: that you, O Lord, would lead me from the unreality of this world we live in, from the tinsel of the things we touch, from its shallowness and superficiality, from all that is cheap, showy, and ostentatious in ourselves and our people. Make me genuine today.
Amen

Thursday
O Lord,
As we believe you are at the door knocking—the church doors, the community doors, the hearts' doors—help us to fling wide the doors of our individual lives, knowing that it all begins or ends right here with me. And bind us all together in ties of love as brothers and sisters.
Amen

Friday
O Lord,
We always come with bundles of expectations, believing that you do great things for us here. We dare to hope because of your promises. Let your Spirit lead us into the truth about ourselves and the truth about the power of your redeeming love.
Amen

Saturday

O Lord,

Your gifts of creation are so rich and full, the glories that we take for granted. Today we stand amazed in the morning sunlight, breathing the fresh air, watching the birds soaring in the clear skies, the leaves blowing in the breezes, and the small creatures that keep it all in order scampering in the underbrush. And we know that we too are intentionally part of this pattern of life, to carry out your creative genius by imitating your caring. Help us today to carefully bring our gifts in love. We ask that you make them a blessing.

Amen

Sunday

O Lord,

You are perfect, complete. When we clamor for some vision, help us to grasp the original recipe, the power of forgiveness, undeserved acceptance, and your demanding righteousness. Remold us today in your image.

Amen

October

WEEK 1

Monday
O Lord,
Walk with me in the plain paths, where the daily routine tests me. If my vision grows dim and my will grows weary, steady my steps. Keep me walking toward the light. Turn me from some dreamy glory to the work of the commonplace, then let me see again the miracles of grace.
Amen

Tuesday
O Lord,
Because you made life out of emptiness, please touch the empty and dying parts of my life. I welcome the abundant life you patiently promised to those who listen, love, and will follow you. Remove my fear of the future, the life that is now, or the life that is yet to be. And let my opening to your Spirit give you freedom to my will, my home, my work, and even my play today.
Amen

Wednesday
O Lord,
In every one of us there is something of you, that image. I claim it today for strength of character, for the power to give, for peace deep inside, that I can feel again the great adventure you made of life. Though I will struggle under a cross, I will know that the path keeps leading upwards. I belong to you: remind me.
Amen

Thursday
O Lord,
I count the blessings you give: health to enjoy, food to savor, friends to share, work to challenge us, faith to practice, life to cherish, hope to guide, joy to carry through our days and beyond. On a clear day like this we can see forever!
Amen

Friday
Use me, Lord!
Your peace has captured me and stilled my fear. Your Spirit makes me strong, and I am ready to listen and to go! Use me today.
Amen

Saturday

O Lord,
You taught us to pray for each other, to give thanks, to confess, to intercede. Where I ask foolish things and omit more important things, remember our childish weakness. Ours is not a praying age, and few of us are deeply praying persons. Hear my groanings between the lines of my prayers. Forgive me and help me pray.
Amen

Sunday

O Lord,
I know you want my heart more than anything else that I may attempt to offer you today. Remind me that you can and will do miracles when I bring you my heart. I am opening that door. Please come in.
Amen

WEEK 2

Monday
O Lord,
I come with so much, while so many come with so little. Make me a giver of the richness of my life, that like good seed, it will grow and spread and bloom into the fruit that makes life—their lives—richer, more peaceful, more decent, and finer as you intended. I pray for them today and for myself.
Amen

Tuesday
O Lord,
I see today how I am surrounded by many good spirits, your work in my life … strong ties of caring; people close like family; people whose quiet humor clears the air; persons enthusiastic about life, themselves, and all that is decent. These make me stronger, and without your mark of mercy, our burden is more than we can bear. Lead me to lead a more thankful life.
Amen

Wednesday
O God,
I confess that I am too busy; that I am set in my ways, not only of good but also of wrong and of half-heartedness; that physical illness troubles me more than spiritual illness; that I say or think awful things of others and discount others deeply. Help me in caring for people, seeing in them what you see.
Amen

Thursday
O Lord,
When I cry for blessings, O Lord, remind me of the blessing just to be alive. What a gift to me. I will breathe deeply, I will look around me, I will think and imagine, and dream, and I will be glad. And yet all else that I wish to have, Lord … Help me claim, grasp, and hold tightly onto a new kind of thankfulness—an active, sweet awareness—for I am alive! Thank you.
Amen

Friday
O Lord,
I've not earned the right to stand before you. I did not just fall into temptation; I went seeking it out. I feel my unworthiness. But look: your outstretched arms, the loving Father welcoming me from the far country! What is it you see in me, in any one of us? And why do you do it? Help me, help any of us, not to count ourselves unworthy of eternity.
Amen

Saturday

Teach me more, O Lord,
The more you teach me about yourself, the more I see my life, my accomplishments, my successes, my possessions as a means to service and less as an end in themselves. Teach me more, Lord, that I can build this pattern in my life.
Amen

Sunday

O Lord,
Your people are quietly slipping in from our often-frantic pace, bent as we are to run ahead of you, wrestling with those commandments and wrenching matters into our own hands that could be better left in yours. Quiet our pulse; restore that jaded spirit. Settle us into trust again. It's your day.
Amen

WEEK 3

Monday

O Lord,

Patient God, I am aware today of my own impatience, so well-honed over years of self-protection. The joy of honest work, the products of what we have done together have given such meaning and a sense of belonging. Help me not to forget this week how you have provided, how lovely and good have been your gifts of providence. Yours, yours alone. Gifts.
Amen.

Tuesday

O Lord,

You were there, not openly changing the circumstances, but just quietly present. This was a crisis and I was frightened, helplessly so, beyond my ability to do more than try a little tenderness. We found resources, we stayed the course without giving up, and you brought peace into that throbbing, incessant pain despite its persistence. You were there. I am living by faith in you.
Amen

Wednesday

O Lord,

I am wondering: Could I be the closed one, who, in clutching my life, may be denying someone else—one close to me or far away—the chance to live fully? Open me, Lord. Where my hands are closed, my heart is shut and my resolve is latched and unexamined. Lead me to give as I have received. You have opened yourself to me.
Amen.

Thursday

O Lord,

I want to let go of the past, but I must not, cannot forget it—its pleasures, its pains, its learnings. Keep me in the faith, bravely, for I am reluctant to keep growing as I might. That first bloom of passion has faded, and I long to move beyond trusting in former days, knowing you are God now, still God tomorrow, and then my God forever.
Amen

Friday

O Lord,

I feel the warmth of today's sunshine, I am surprised by the fragrance of flowers, I hear the laughter of the children and the chattering of old people walking, and I know how rich I am to have a happy, grateful heart.
Amen

Saturday

O Happy Day,
When you took me in and made me yours!
Amen

Sunday

Lord,
Make us instruments of your peace. Where there is hatred, let us sow love; where there is injury, pardon; where there is conflict, peace; where there is doubt, faith; where there is despair, hope; where there is darkness, light; where there is sadness, joy. Grant that we may not so much seek to be consoled as to console, to be understood as to understand, to be loved as to love. For it is in giving that we receive; it is in pardoning that we are pardoned; it is in dying that we are born to eternal life.
Amen

WEEK 4

Monday
O Lord of life,
While I beg for some morsel of your attention … If it were not for the warmth of sunlight, the rain that washed the land, the green earth drenched in dew, the moonlit night weaving its delicate magic, the hushed hours of quiet joy, the triumphs of my soul matched by the clutches of sorrow when I feel "the everlasting arms," I would be an aimless wanderer. How marvelous is grace, your loving kindness!
Amen

Tuesday
O Lord,
You are the God of the impossible, and I am only growing to understand that. My prayer of faith is my sense of expectation, but in prayer I admit I do not know what love can or cannot do. Help me, Lord, for prayer is still at best a growing edge, and I will keep on praying.
Amen

Wednesday
O Lord,
God of promises, unfailingly you gather people in, bind us up together, and then bless us with hope and graces and spirit. All this because burdens are borne invisibly, sorrows are unseen but so heavy, and our errors are deep with shame. Save me from a tepid faith that is only thoughts and prayers. Save me for a faith ready with a clear mind, listening ears, and outstretched hands.
Amen

Thursday
O Lord,
You speak and with your words you create. Speaking is one of the tools of our lives, and a tool of trade for me. And I speak more than I want, randomly, constantly, garrulous at times, creating what I do not want. Lord, help me control my speech and my tongue. I pray you will help me to speak with words worthy of these important days.
Amen

Friday
O Lord,
I love baseball, and I hope you do because the World Series games are captivating. I love their skillful determination, such youthful energies and dedicated excitement. The roaring crowd on a few acres of high hopes makes expectations of championship play sky high. What if we had a World Series of prayer, not for competition but for all-out pulling the plug on outstanding

performance, with everybody winning this game? And it feels so much like a game sometimes, and our team is not looking like the winners. Do you love baseball? Then why not? Why not?
Amen

Saturday

O Lord,

I enjoyed a genuine friend this week, and I was rather caught by surprise. It was a crisis that brought us together, and he needed a friend. I had the resources and the heart that he needed today, though I hardly knew it. What a sweet experience. This was grace in reverse. Thank you, Lord, for this surprise and for the grace that seems to always be enough for us all.
Amen

Sunday

O Lord,

Magnificent Artist, the whole earth is shouting your colorful and joyful spirit. It looks and sounds like a church on Sunday, or what I imagine your people really might be when gathered up and full of your story. O make us like that, this morning, full of your story, and full of your colorful, surprising exuberance.
Amen

November

WEEK 1

Monday
O Lord,
There is so much confusion that has led so many astray, wandering around and going nowhere. It's a judgement on our harsh theology, our stern exclusiveness. It's a harsh regime at times, and so many have run away, sadly. Teach us, urge us, help us to say, "Our Father," and "Forgive them," again and again and again. Help us to keep the light on in the window for them this week.
Amen

Tuesday
O Lord,
You gave us David and Goliath as a story for our time: giants threaten the peace of the world still. Even faith takes up stones to fight now as then. Speak to me now, that I will not wear the armor of my opponent, but live by whom and what I know to be true.
Amen

Wednesday
O Lord,
Grace: I hear so much that I take it for granted, presuming the meaning without being clear on it. It is meant to penetrate my protective defenses, isn't it? And it doesn't help much where it does not. But today when I was caught doing wrong, and now as I hear about grace, when I need it most … I find you looking beyond my outward embarrassment and reaching for and touching my heart instead. Now I understand. How can I say thanks? Amen

Thursday
O Lord,
Winning is a phenomenon we ourselves have created, pushing competition, the means to best someone. Your sweet achievement is open to all of us, just to not quit, something called always doing your best and never giving up. Faithfulness: It's open to us all, all the time. There's no shame in that achievement. Your victory is sweet for us all.
Amen

Friday
O Lord,
Grace: You sent it not as an agent to destroy and shame, but as a means to set us free, to enable me to become a man after God's own heart, and I want that more than anything. I hunger for it. I wait for more.
Amen

Saturday

O Lord,

You are the Lord of opportunity. From someone's best desires a family has been formed, a church has been born, a ministry idea has found its targets, a hospital was built, a mission was performed, and someone was healed. Another was given hope, another given a friend, a child a home with parents. A fellowship found purpose and love. A dream went from thoughts and prayers to a real shape of faith at work. Make my faith work, and trust me with an opportunity, too, please.

Amen

Sunday

O Lord,

Will you make my life a genuine channel for your love to all the people I live around? Can you do that? And if you uncover blind prejudices and lurking, smoldering grudges that keep your love from finding a way to someone who needs it, I will promise to give you a free hand to clean it out, and I do ask for you to forgive me.

Amen

WEEK 2

Monday
O Lord,
In your patience you give us time, and I thank you for it. Learning to intertwine my time with others is like the flowering around the dilapidated home of my life, time over coffee, time in the common tasks, kids' time, music-listening time, times of resting, holy time, and a time to catch my breath. Help me find a pace I can hold, that I may endure, that I may laugh, that I may believe beyond the grave.
Amen

Tuesday
O Lord,
Laboring in your world takes patience that I need and I pray for today. The reward is so good, the joy of honesty, the pride in the products of what I have done, the sense of meaning and belonging, the being a part of something bigger than myself, and of being a part of other people's lives, then knowing you do not forget what we have done. Help me get home in time for supper!
Amen

Wednesday
O Lord,
Forgive me when I demand flesh-and-blood signs of you to be sustained on my journey. I am hungrily seeking what is sacred within the ordinary. I still want burning bushes, falling quail, mysterious manna. Help me as I keep on developing spiritual sensitivity that I can find you again, knitting up the unraveled wounds of this human dilemma.
Amen

Thursday
O Lord,
I heard they called the old saint "Camel Knees." He had such callouses from his praying. Lord, I want to be like that. Give me camel knees. Help me believe and pray like that.
Amen

Friday
O Lord,
My prayer is like a hike in high mountains. All I see is the road. The land is like a shadow dance, then stops quickly and the sky is clear again. Exposed, the wind of the Spirit can knock me down. I step onto the ridge, and a blast of air nearly carries me away. I have dismissed the altitude, and I feel I am in trouble. Help me! My need is so great. Yet my search is genuine because my trouble is greater. This walk is far too treacherous to take alone. Lead me, Lord.
Amen

Saturday

O Lord,

I come alone, up a jagged peak where many others greater than I have climbed many times before. I am reaching for you, Lord. The bright sky overhead grows suddenly dark. This prayer is a remote place for me. I feel lost in a distant haze, but the summit, the moments of assurance of your hearing, your answering, is calling me. Take my hand.
Amen

Sunday

O Lord,

As I pray this morning, I know I am just another one in a land of prodigious talkers. Yet I come knowing you are the absolute mightiest. Show me again today how to listen. You have invited me into your presence like into my homeland. Lord, I come.
Amen

WEEK 3

Monday
O Lord,
As I look around at my neighbors, how easy to see them as a congregation, just another varied collection of people of many thoughts and life commitments—just neighbors, just my brothers and sisters, but so much your children. I want to love like you love. Make my lovingkindness be like yours for them.
Amen

Tuesday
O Lord,
I like to be an encourager—like a full cup overflowing, sometimes splashing and sloshing out, other times gently spilling over. And everybody needs it, deserves it, hungers for just a little recognition of what they're trying to do and to be. Fill me, use me, and thank you for sharing the energy and the joy.
Amen

Wednesday
O Lord,
Seeing and hearing the stories of people who have lived selflessly, filled with courage and at great cost, I weep. I am humbled beyond repair. I know how I have failed you over and over, and worse, I know you know. O how deep is my despair. I bow my head in shame. What could possibly change this deep sadness before you? God's gonna trouble the water.
Amen

Thursday
O Lord,
"Traveling mercies," they ask. "Be with him," they say. These are what you pledged already. Why do we plead like this? Make my prayers a meaningful cry … for daily provisions and needs as you have taught me … about daily bread, about forgiveness, about steering me from temptation. Make my prayers a real cry to heaven for more than security, but for living to the utmost for your highest—an effort to call upon you in my genuine need.
Amen

Friday
O Lord,
We all have a story, and I know you know every single one, and you know mine. I want to take the time to know those stories of my friends. So many twists and turns in their lives have made them who they are, the interesting and yet complicated conglomeration of all that has formed

their lives. What a wonder lies within each of our lives, and you know every portion—big and small. And I want to know more of your story, too, Lord.
Amen

Saturday

O Lord,
O God of all creation, owner of all things, your riches are evident in the greatest and the smallest parts of our world. It is all yours. We are the users as you intended. Sometimes I am astonished at how we all grab for more and more so we can be rich. We seem to stop at nothing to get our cut, cheating each other, greedily like pigs. O Lord, save me from my own bent toward cheating my fellow brothers and sisters.
Amen

Sunday

O Lord,
I have shared time with a person who is almost 100, yet full to overflowing of life and purpose and desire. Such is the gift of walking a lifetime with Almighty God of purposeful love. You fill us up with life, and you give us all a reason, a purpose for living. Fill me again, Lord!
Amen

WEEK 4

Monday

O Lord,
I wept today, overcome by love, by the sense of your surrounding presence. To pray can be so sweet like that. To know that you know me and you still care about me. And I know it and can feel it.
Amen

O Lord,
I celebrate your artistry in this changing weather, its unvarnished beauty, its magical dependability, its call to my soul to move with its seasonally evolving life, its slow march to its next moments. In it all, somehow, I feel the resounding truth that you are indeed unchanging, ever the same—yesterday, today, tomorrow, and forever. Anchor my life in you, Lord, as I move into the unceasing movement toward tomorrow.
Amen

Tuesday

O God of power,
How often I come to you for power—power over my circumstances, power over my enemies, even disease, and power over myself. But how powerless I can feel sometimes when praying through impossible odds. I only ask that you give me the power that never fails, the power to keep on believing. Amen

Wednesday

O Lord,
What do I do when I am so angry? A gentler spirit would not take offense so easily, I know. It's when I reach my limit and I can take no more; when I feel all alone, excluded, different, and "unrespected." Is it my time to be respectful, and am I the one who needs to give? Is that to turn the other cheek? Is that the way? With your help I can know and do what I should be doing.
Amen

Thursday

O Lord,
I live in the midst of my scatteredness, pulled in so many directions, filling the empty time-slots with entertainment. Reconnect me, reshape me, help me care enough, try enough, to notice and to do enough that I might be a genuine encourager beyond "generic positivity."
Amen

Friday

O Lord,
I have hungered all week for I don't know what. I have been telling you all week what I need. That's it, isn't it, a me-centered prayer, telling you what I want, passing that off for prayer? I give you my frustration, heaving deeply. I still my thoughts and get quiet. Let me be simple, grateful for your companionship again, that which I have forgotten. Be still and know.
Amen

Saturday

O Lord,
I feel like I am too busy to pray today, but I will pray out of a discipline well learned. If I were to pray to you from my feelings, it would be anemic, sporadic at best. At worst I would be demanding some answers I have never yet found. Are you running with me, Jesus? Some answers would help, so help me to see them.
Amen

Sunday

O Lord,
There is a gripping drama in your unfolding story, and today I will be told again that I have a role in it. That demands both my faith and my reason, and I long to be ready. Show me the path, and order my steps today.
Amen

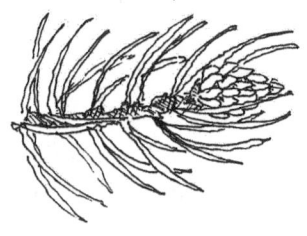

WEEK 5

Monday
O Lord,
We saw a lady weeping as she walked away from the cash register, and we were dumbstruck watching her fail to match her food stamps bill. She could not take her groceries. The lady behind her insisted on paying the tab! We all choked with surprise, and I felt you weeping too. I know you are teaching me every day about riches, reminding me what it means to love enough.
Amen

Tuesday
O God of power,
Come to me here and get down below the surface of my skin. Release me from the confines of my everydayness. There is more of me down here, but I struggle to get to it and let it live. My spiritual callouses are from a brand of institutional faith that stops seeking you. Meet me here, Lord, I pray.
Amen

Wednesday
O Lord,
I'm finding it disarmingly easy to go on "auto pilot" in my prayers! I don't want to wait for something to grab my attention. I am fully here, crying out to you, fully present listening, remembering, counting up, ready for this moment! I give myself into you now.
Amen

Thursday
O Lord,
This day, to count the blessings of the year is such a national treasure. Create in me today that radiant and beautiful humility so precious to you, a gratefulness that shows itself like an abundant and colorful garden facing heavenward, an attitude and a spirit that draw something quietly beautiful in spirit from the others with whom I will share this day. Draw from us then the happy gratitude you deserve.
Amen

Friday
O Lord,
It's people I pray for today—my friends, my brothers and sisters, remarkable examples of busy lives. There is so much you have to give them, and what you give is so liberating. And that's exactly what they are yearning for. How frustrating to have only my own self to be able to control and direct. I must do more, a better job within my own life, all I can, if you will help me. All I have to offer to them is what I can prove in me. Be my strength as you are my hope.
Amen

Saturday

O Lord,

How stark is the contrast between honesty and dishonesty, painfully distant from each other, and clearly evident in the eyes, pointing all the way down into the soul. How sweet, refreshing, and reassuring is the one; how painful to watch is the other. Lord, am I an honest one? Thoroughly and purely honest? Even translucent down to a soul that reveals how good and peaceful it is to be unreservedly honest? Don't let me be just honest enough, but honest, with peace in my soul, at peace with my Creator.

Amen

Sunday

To love our God, the reason we live;
To love our God, the highest goal.
For to satisfy the soul,
For its meaning makes us whole
For the purpose we were made …
To love our God!
Amen
(By Mark Hayes)

December

WEEK 1

Monday

O Lord of promises,
You made a life-sized covenant with us, with this whole world. And before the ink was dry, we were off to try our luck at running things our way. What astounding carelessness in the very arms of such world-sized care! When will we ever learn to rest in your care without fear? There's no losing our opportunities to stand on those promises. Lord, have mercy.
Amen

Tuesday

O Lord,
There is joy in knowing you, joy to the world. How much we need it, for all the people of the world. Let me bear the news, not the giddy feeling, but the news of a great God whose love knows no bounds.
Amen

Wednesday

O Lord,
I know this faith is no counterfeit, living just for today alone. This trusting in you is only underway, for I can see you removing tears and death and planning the life where there will be no evil. Lift me up to celebrating this reminder that you have been at this grace for a long time and have given me a promise to continue for generations to come.
Amen

Thursday

O Lord,
This season of thankfulness slides too easily into the disorder of dissatisfaction. We know how precarious life is. We know and feel the threat of unfulfilled hopes and dreams, of personal calamity, of political catastrophe. But this faith you have given us is this: that you are for us; that you plan our lives; that you direct the nations. Give me courage to walk this path of God!
Amen

Friday

O Lord,

I believe! I trust you, completely! I see the wonders of your love working through the committed lives of the people all around me who love you and live as you have led us. The pieces of life come falling into place as if parts of a grand puzzle, and the blessed people around us handle each part, carefully laying them in place, fitting them together, bringing a lovely picture of life that surely must please you gloriously. This I believe and thrill to the joy of believing.

Amen

Saturday

O Lord,

Believing has transformed my mind and heart. I am at peace; it is peace with you, peace by living in you, peace deep inside, and a confident calm come what may. What a gift! From this peace I can act with confident strength to help bring about the good that we were created for. This is really living!

Amen

Sunday

O Lord of Rest,

I thank you for our time together; for quieting my spirit with a word of assurance and hope; for time to think, to plan, to hope, to warm to a better idea, to enjoy a cup of coffee. May I arise to be of some usefulness. And I pray for people faithfully tending others' lives: that they might find a pace they can hold, that they may endure, that they may laugh, that they may believe beyond the grave.

Amen

WEEK 2

Monday
O Lord,
I saw a man who could not breathe today, overweight, struggling to get from room to room, and he told me his story. It is one of abuse, from early days at home, right through growing up, through the service to his country, leading to his own continuation of a terrible pattern of abuse to himself. We have this raw violence in our land of enormous proportion, and the times have found us! How can we ask to be forgiven for what we have ignored? O God, help us.
Amen

Tuesday
O Lord,
I saw a prissy, perfect, and proud lady today. She was dressed so well—perfectly appointed with jewelry, hair, and makeup—and driving a fine car. She brought in her promised support, the stuff that makes our caring work possible. I heard reports of her faithful work and her faithful life. I had wanted to be judgmental—that is, until I felt your love for her. Forgive me, Lord, for I know not what I'm doing.
Amen

Wednesday
O Lord,
Praying today, I tried the hasp and it would not move, a familiar gate I have used before but now locked up tight from disuse. There was a sign saying to go around to another entrance, but I was too tired to try. I wanted to go in my way. I was the loser today, the petulant, demanding child. I had an airtight argument. You gently showed me the way and waited while I pouted and walked away.
Amen

Thursday
O Lord,
I am awash in guilt and shame of past mistakes and prideful unwillingness to make those necessary changes pledged on blended knee. Surely your grace and persistence can one day destroy every vestige of "the old regime." I know you can and surely in your way and your time you will. I rest my heart, trusting you this morning.
Amen

Friday

O Lord,

I keep hearing the call from the wildly shouting prophet, "Repent!" but preparing for the season is the main demand now. We have friends to see, groups to gather up for celebration, baking of all the expected goodies and deliveries, great meals to plan, and the party! It all takes so much time to pull together. So, let's put off these aged calls of the prophets. I will get to the religious parts of this season soon enough, I think. I do have a favorite nativity scene.
Amen

Saturday

O Lord,

In lovingkindness you provide so quietly and so generously, with beautiful thoroughness. All nature is yours. All creation is your handiwork, not mine. I bow my head to receive your goodness in simple thankfulness. Give me one thing more: a pure heart.
Amen

Sunday

O Lord,

In worship I am given the blessing I do not deserve: your presence in my heart, your promises on my life, your love surrounding me in full assurance. Help me to keep on learning to bless other people—all people—and not to judge.
Amen

WEEK 3

Monday
O Lord,
I have heard there is good news: Everything is on sale! Now we can get more and have more and more, and people won't be denied anything we want. Rejoice in the good news! New cars are available, and that says "Joy to the World." How good. It's been a desert down here. Thanks.
Amen

Tuesday
O Lord,
While waiting for dinner out, a celebrity noticed us—and spoke to us! What a nice surprise for the season. Last month he took his life. Who can imagine what despair lurks behind every face, every heart? But you see it all and know every secret. If only I had known, I might have offered a word of hope, because you have given me that. If only I had known...
Amen

Wednesday
O Lord,
There is so much food, food, food everywhere, and I am about to pop! Dinners with neighbors, and cookies, cakes, breads, goodies, cheese and crackers, cider, and wines. How good when generosity fills the air and we put differences aside and learn to laugh at ourselves again! It is jolly when little grievances find their right perspective and we share and hum and sing, decorate and plan, nibble and make wishes. Truly we should fear not. I'm about to pop because I am not used to this. Teach me again to fear not.
Amen

Thursday
O Lord,
How I see again that my thoughts are not your thoughts. Where you use innocence, this world has regarded it as subversive, seditious, revolutionary to the powers in this world. Where I want fairness for my dollars, you throw your weight against the privileged who have so much and press the cause of those victims of my society who have so little, who cannot get a fair day in court, who are exploited by scheming money lenders, for aliens who are seen only as a cheap source of labor. I cry out for impartiality, and you are showing all of us what that really means. Lord, you are not sentimental with me today; you are tough as nails.
Amen

Friday

O Lord,

You know I hate to be in this shopping spree. And as I sing the hymns of Christmas, I long for the holy kindness of the season. I'll string lights in the darkening days and give the gifts of the stories that have touched me deeply this year. But in truth, something of now does not easily package up. I feel so deeply that I must give myself to you again. Lead me, Lord. I need your hand again.

Amen

Saturday

O Lord,

Friends are your best gifts, Lord, persons who stop to talk, who look me in the eye, who seem to listen with understanding, who tell me something good, who take time and hand it off without the packaging of loose rattling anxieties, whose smiles are genuine and lovely and whose help is ready and offered without asking. These are instructors of faith, demonstrators of peace, harbingers of hopefulness, and they betray a joy deeper than a surface-textured attempt at good spirits. They point me to you. Thank you.

Amen

Sunday

O Lord of promises,

You made a life-sized covenant with us, with this whole world. But before the ink was dry, we were off to try our luck at running things our way. What astounding carelessness in the very arms of such world-sized care. When will we ever learn to rest in your care without fear? There's no losing our opportunities to stand on those promises. Lord have mercy.

Amen

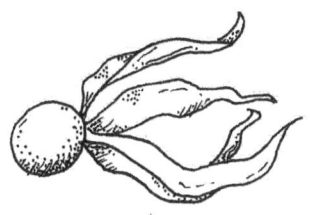

WEEK 4

Monday

O Lord,

Do they hear what I hear? The news is everywhere. There is great joy a'coming! One day all people everywhere will see you, God. They will know you, Lord. They will know the truth, clearly before their very eyes, and be set free. Is it too good to be true? I am hoping that it's true, counting on it! That's a great joy!

Amen

Tuesday

O Lord,

There is life-changing power in friendship! To think that you did that, you gave us that! How can I do less?

Amen

Wednesday

O Lord,

I've never been good at birthdays. In fact, I never remember dates. But this one is how the world keeps track of the arrival of the one thing that gives us hope in the midst of despair, joy in the soul of monotony, peace in a world of confusion, love as an answer in a defiant and destructive world-spirit of power, greed, and selfish demands to choose the wrong regardless of everything right. I am so grateful to remember.

Amen

Thursday

O Lord,

After all the festivity, the nativity, the passing brevity, I pray that this message gets out; that it lingers on our hearts; that it draws from this world of people gifts that carry this message of life and love far beyond our small borders. And show me how to carry this light and carry it better than before.

Amen

Friday

O Lord,

Gifts and giving characterize this season for all of us, no matter our stripe. It tells the world so subtly of your nature: giving, generously, graciously, regardless of our deserving. Never let me take these gifts for granted: *hope* in this world; *peace* so purposeful, plentiful, and for everyone; *joy* as simple as a baby's cry; and the *love* that gives freedom when it is accepted and received. These gifts never grow old. What a God of such grace!

Amen

Saturday

O Lord,

Believing, just embracing the simple story—your story, O Lord—like a hungry person takes bread because they need it and want it so badly, because they're hungry. Believing creates a sense of wonder, without which no one will enter your circle, your family, your gathering of the beloved. Oh Joy, the freedom that comes in accepting and believing! Such a calling to life. I believe; help me where I do not believe.

Amen

Sunday

O Lord,

Knowing you, there is so much joy that sometimes I think I might just burst! Yet I fear I only misrepresent your magnificence, your creative perfection, your overshadowing love. O Great Creator, give me fearless abandon, but mold me into the winsome image of your determined and purposeful love.

Amen

January

WEEK 1

Monday
O Lord,
I see the old tree out front is leaning over, it's limbs once sprawling and shading us all, are now broken and falling, spilling over the ground. Its life has been legendary among us and now it is bare and old. So, like our lives you have given us, we grow old and loose the strength we once had, our useful days are past. I will cherish the old ones and drop seeds for new ones to come after me. It is your plan, your way, Lord, and I will do as you have planned and be glad.
Amen

Tuesday
O Lord,
I have shared time with a person who is almost one hundred, yet full to overflowing of life and purpose and desire. Such is the gift of walking a lifetime with Almighty God of purposeful love. You fill us up with life, and you give us all a reason, a purpose for living! Fill me again, Lord!
Amen

Wednesday
O Lord,
It happened when I was not looking or just did not notice. The amaryllis bloomed, so did the sprawling Christmas cactus, and the fragrant paper whites, and the unexpected kalanchoe, all broke forth with new life, brilliant with colorful surprise, perfectly shaped and reaching forward for light. Someone else was tending, watching, preparing. Someone else had provided and I am in awe. O make me not so demanding to know and understand, but to joyfully expect, to accept, to wait patiently, to believe again!
Amen

Thursday
O Lord,
For forever I have heard your voice. By those beloved scriptures spoken and I learned, you guided me, admonished and corrected. The times are dark, and we need that clarion word from you to push back the darkness, to light the way. Speak, please. I pray for a word discernible, not hidden, for our sight is dimming.
Amen

Daily Prayers

Friday

O Lord,

A new year brings new thoughts and hopefully new ways. With new insights you give and new paths I can expect new directions, a new me. I want to leave behind the sloppy slide into the easy- not the faithful- way. I want to embrace the miserable discomfort I feel as your dissatisfaction when I chose the lesser way. I want to celebrate each time my strength comes from letting your Spirit guide. Let me not merely hate what is evil, strengthen and reshape me to love what is good, with all my heart!

Amen

Saturday

O Lord,

Peace and good will were announced as the results of your saving grace, so the process of making peace should be comparatively easy, a recognized fact. That is the commonsense view. But those of us who get comfortable at the top seldom appreciate what ordinary people have so desperately needed. Forgive us, Lord, and knowing our war is won, help us with vision and courage not to lose it again at the peace table.

Amen

Sunday

O Lord,

I entered the church, the big one, the Basilica. It had a "Cry Room," upstairs for little ones. I need a sign for the big room for we big people need to cry. Another church might have said, "Stop your crying. Come in and feel good." Hurts and fears silenced, confusions denied. I know you bear my sorrows and carry my shame. You do it with me, lifting me so beautifully, and you do it for me when I cannot.

Amen

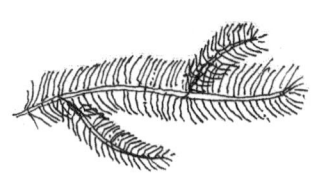

WEEK 2

Monday
O Lord,
I hear a lot of the short answers, and I bet you do, too. "It's fine!" "I'm good." "We're done." "No, uh uh." Short answers just don't settle the big questions. Our issues of life are not that easy. Are these then the brush off, a signal that we don't want to be bothered? I know I whine ofttimes, but please don't stop bothering me, Lord. I need your wisdom. "Thy Word is a lamp unto my feet and a light unto my path!"
Amen

Tuesday
O Lord,
Most folks keep up and stay engaged by reading their newspaper, so I left out early to get mine! Early is such a nice and unique time of day, and it belongs to the focused and the determined. I like being among them, they have much to say about how the day will turn out, each day being a gift they seem to appreciate and receive so willingly and gladly. I sat and watched a few busily getting their early starts, and one had a limp. He seemed almost more determined and prouder than most, headed into the store to start the day. And many of us have a limp, most, I believe, and we are most determined, because we believe you are determined.
Amen

Wednesday
O Lord,
Are we looking for dignity in all the wrong places? When church as we know it is being replaced by cultural shifts, I see restaurants provide the happy gathering, fitness offer challenging discipline, and sports bringing active team learning. All these my church once gave me with wonderfully warm and inspiring teachers. Are you building a new kind of church, or are we just dismantling what you did right a generation ago? Show me so I can join in!
Amen

Thursday
O Lord,
I am a believer! I am yours! Body and soul! How sweet it is...to belong. Everybody needs a friend, a purpose, and to belong to something! And I have that, as I have this faith, what you have so carefully, generously given. I believe, and so I live. And for those loose ends, where I fail to let it show...help Thou mine unbelief!
Amen

Friday

O Lord,
I saw the old grouch again, and I think he enjoys being miserable! My days of wishing him to be miserable just made me more so. It isn't working. Now I have seen him different, broken, hurting, afraid and in need of a friend. I can do that because you taught me how when you befriended me. I didn't deserve it then either.
Amen

Saturday

O Lord,
How do you beat selfishness? It is one of the strongest survival techniques we have, and it works, works wonders, when trying just to keep your head above waters. But I know it is addictive. It is a heady medicine, and it grabs something deep inside that is beyond my knowing! Lord, help save me from this delicious brew, so easily seen in others but easily ignored in me! Help me!
Amen

Sunday

O Lord,
To live by faith I need a message of hope to beat this spiritual vacuum of today! Our generation is putting you, O Lord, in a box, refusing to acknowledge any supernatural powers that cannot be explained or proven. "Why accommodate what is invisible?" But nothing in this world of ours is permanent. "I wanna be in the world where it happens!" Where you are...where you restore the broken, heal our diseases, reassure our weak hearts and guide us by faith! Keep me there!
Amen

WEEK 3

Monday

O Lord,

I have a friend who carves gourds, gorgeous, colorful, with deep meanings and significance, then gives them away! He was a judge who carved the beautiful, lifesaving law on people's lives from his chamber and bench. This is his retirement new avocation and artwork. O make my prayers in my retirement as beautiful, redeeming, colorful and life affirming for other people as the gourds of my friend!

Amen

Tuesday

O Lord,

My friend called and spoke of peace, wishing peace upon me. He who had been to war and fought and served so well, who knew the price of wars and had paid the price and genuinely had a deeper peace within himself. I open myself, mind and heart to you, knowing this peace is not a product to be purchased but a gift of your love, a relationship, not a platform to look at but an experience of your acceptance of me just as I am. I open myself again to you, gladly.

Amen

Wednesday

O Lord,

I thank you for the morning light and evening peace, for the night in which you have restored my spirit's strength and the day in which you lead me into a larger life, for the past that gives me such a blessing and the future to which I lift my eyes in hope. O Lord you are my strength, my joy and my hope.

Amen

Thursday

O Lord,

My friend was alone so I came to visit and we talked for hours! I did not realize that loneliness was so deadening and so deadly. I was humbled to listen to so much life, humbled to be her friend, humbled to be given such a gift of her time. I had forgotten that time multiplies when given away, forgotten what a life-giving gift you created and entrusted to every one of us. Help me not to waste or to lose even one precious second.

Amen

Friday

O Lord,
A new kind of Christian, they say. Can we successfully modernize a timeless classic? Could it run the thin line between blasphemy and anachronism? Basking in the rosy glow of nostalgia, we Christians mostly stand ready to crucify the new product, or at least exclude them from our regular churches. Lord, do you fear the loss of the original recipe as I do? Order our steps with your word!
Amen

Saturday

O Lord,
"Tis the gift to be simple, tis the gift to be free, tis the gift to turn round like we ought to be!" And you showed how when we willingly admit our faults and turn round. Simplicity is truly needed by our generation. Oh how complex we have made it when pride gets in the way! Let me be simple enough to admit my wrongs and be free and be joyful.
Amen

Sunday

O Lord,
I have hungered all week for I don't know what. I have been telling you all week what I need. That's it, isn't it, a me-centered prayer, telling you what I want, passing that off for prayer. I give you my frustration, heaving deeply, I still my thoughts and get quiet. Let me be simple, grateful for your companionship again, that which I have forgotten. Be still and know...
Amen

WEEK 4

Monday
O Lord,
It grieves me that the talking heads of TV and name brand religion are "controlling the narrative" about my God! I long to hear the sweet, sweet song of salvation. O how we need those prophets of old, brave and sure, speaking the music of your sweet mercy again. Send us many who will bring your message again to the sick and hungry rather than just to the well fed.
Amen

Tuesday
O Lord,
"The readiness is all!" I know you are above it all and with me in it all! I confess my fretting and despair when times are difficult, my temptation to say and do rash things and forgetting that both light and darkness are the same to you. Now I place my most poignant hours in your hands. I surrender my hurts to your wisdom, and prepare myself for your divine appointments. And I say, yes!
Amen

Wednesday
O Lord,
Faith, tiny like a mustard seed, even that will move a mountain? I must be reminded, because often to have only a tiny speck, a flickering light threatened by every wind of disappointment, holding only a speck of the once driving force of my life is discouraging, demeaning at best. Oh stir those dying embers into a flaming torch! I cry out to you like Sampson did, blinded by his foolish pride, but crying for one more chance to see!
Amen

Thursday
O Lord,
Some truly remarkable servants of yours are living way up in years. Where is the plan for those who live so long, living alone, struggling alone with their health and the necessary care? When haunted by a diminishing sense of purpose? These have not outlived their usefulness, so help me be a reminder of the plan and purpose they so crave, that your loving kindness is better than life itself!
Amen

Friday

O Lord,

Some truly remarkable servants of yours are living way up in years. Where is the plan for those who live so long, living alone, struggling alone with their health and the necessary care? When haunted by a diminishing sense of purpose? These have not outlived their usefulness, so help me be a reminder of the plan and purpose they so crave, that your loving kindness is better than life itself!

Amen

Saturday

O Lord,

I've seen pride raise its unbending head, refusing to share, snubbing a chance to participate and be counted, rejecting any help, denying the importance, laughing and shrugging, but I saw the fear lurking behind the mask. Afraid, like a wounded child. The hardening of the heart is a sad thing to watch. Is there is a point where it is irreversible, when I care so much, and it grieves me so? My heart is broken and I feel yours is too, but won't give up because I know you never do.

Amen

Sunday

O Lord,

"...worship in the beauty of Holiness." I have to be literally tripped up to remember you are a God of perfect goodness, perfection, breathtakingly beautiful, what a vision of your true self. I am now renewed by that quality of your penetrating mercy and your graceful forgiveness and love, and now challenged by your demanding righteousness.

Amen

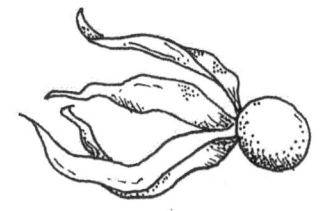

WEEK 5

Monday

O Lord,
Be persistent today, Lord. Give me no rest until I am willing to rest in you. Be active and present anywhere and everywhere. Without you I can do nothing. With you I can do all things!
Amen

Tuesday

O Lord,
The neighbors got together, and I walked among them and smiled as I watched them all. Before me stood a library of story after story, everyone different and each one unique, and I wondered, was anyone else reading as I was. We all had written and you had inspired, supplied, watched, encouraged and loved. I, too, loved and wished I could read every word as you have. And you know the conclusion of each one. Each started with love, and each will end with love.
Amen

Wednesday

O Lord,
How wonderful to be loved by you, knowing your love is never limited to a certain kind, or restricted to our kind, but extended to all, all, the dependent, the desperate, the determined, for I am all of these at times. You are calling all of us to stretch to that high position, to love you back with all, with all my heart, my soul, my mind, my strength. Thank you for calling me today into your belonging love. May all of me be yours, not just part of me. Help me to be the wholehearted one you created me to be, and then be made whole!
Amen

Thursday

O Lord,
Whenever I am afraid, I hear your story again, and I hold my head up high. You came to destroy evil, and make me your child, an heir. When with this hope I purify myself as you are pure, I become like you. When you come again in power, I will be made like you. Forgive me if this sounds trite, but now I whistle a happy tune!
Amen

Friday

O Lord,
"Ain't got much hope these days…but I'll do what I can." The wonder that captured me is that you reveal yourself…in love, in power, in purposeful perfection. Do it again, Lord! There is an emptiness that only you can fill. Our new generation is in such need, we all are. Do it again!
Amen

Saturday

O Lord,
Oh this faith is good! What a sure hope, startling me back in the darkest times. Lord keep me trusting, believing...in the family of your beloved, the washing of my sins, the resurrection to new life, and the clear guiding of your Spirit! What a real and sure hope! I am real and full of hope!
Amen

Sunday

O Lord,
I went to church and I wondered, did they know you were there? I was quieted, and in hushed awe, I knew you were there. Did they know? Was it different for others as it was for me? Why didn't they stay a little longer? I only left because it was over, but I gladly would have stayed and stayed and stayed.
Amen

February

WEEK 1

Monday

O Lord,
"Faith is the victory!" Yes, it is true, for faith in you has given me unexpectedly a life of hope filled courage, an abundant life. There are those gifts of essential energy and vision, the freedoms of honesty and purity, the joys of brothers and sisters of the heart, and that incredible inward peace, though sometimes rising and falling as it is. Beautiful, and how can I say thanks.
Amen

Tuesday

O Lord,
The challenge of my faith is not merely believing in things and in you, for I can counsel myself back into that when I seem to be slipping. The challenge is to let it be your gift rather than my work, my effort, something I achieve. I need the simplicity of little children, the clear and simple laughter from being free, the giggles of being surprised again, those little legs that dance and jump and run and never stand still, the simplicity of smiles, hugs, even tears and quick recoveries. Help me to "Be still and know…"
Amen

Wednesday

O Lord,
My friend is dying. She has made all of her arrangements, and she is not afraid, neither am I. But, oh the hurt has left me crying and broken. I am too tender, much too broken for these moments, these losses. Why? Why have you made me this way? I only want to pray that all this will go away, but I sense it is your way. I do tell friends, "God removes all fear!" yet that God fills that space with tender devotion, all wrapped up in hopes, for those who will call upon You. They may cry, too, while they hope in you.
Amen

Thursday

O Lord,
Forgiveness is so hard. How do you do it? We cannot let them run over us! You did it and at what a price! The sting hurts, the insult makes a scar, a constant reminder. I could hide. I could pretend it's not there, but then its cesspool of unfinished business will remind me. How did you do it? This is your work, your identifying character. I remember now, I am the one to be forgiven. Now I understand. Now I can do it. Thank you.
Amen

Friday

O Lord,

Honesty is a precious commodity and costly at times. I have seen it make heroes of the simplest ones of us. With it you build community, even your sacred family of the beloved. Forgive me when I fail to recognize the opportunities you give to live it, to love it, recognize it, cherish it and protect it. It shows when we are free and keeps us free, and by it we keep faith with you and with our brothers and sisters. You first showed it and taught it to me in Eden of Genesis.
Amen

Saturday

O Lord,

Teach me to pray prayers that deserve to be heard. I don't ask that you make me better than other people, just better than myself, changed from what I am to what I ought to be. Shine the light on what is dark within and raise up high what is sagging and low within me. Whatever I am, past, present, or future, I know your greatness and goodness are always sufficient.
Amen

Sunday

O Lord,

"To love our God, the reason we live…" Musically it is beautiful, but practically so challenging as to scare so many of us away. But the beauty, the freedom, the abundance awaits any who hear that first and greatest commandment. Never let me stray far from this call to really living, for it is the reason you have given me to live, today and always.
Amen

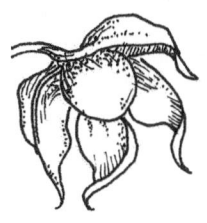

WEEK 2

Monday

O Lord,

The world is wild and unpredictable, but many people find that sports offer a world that is orderly and fair. In the world there are rules, some written, some understood and unwritten, but rules so often ignored by many as if they were optional. The rules of sports are closely monitored, protective, agreed upon by all players, and provide a good time for all. Many people who can't handle the unpredictable find solace, opportunity, and a safe place in sports, a world of skill to be admired and discipline to be celebrated, a world open to all who will play by the rules. The world is reality, open to all, to be used, abused, or cherished and treasured. Life is precious. Handle with care.

Amen

Tuesday

O Lord,

I have so much and so much gratitude wells up in my heart. I have the strength and energy and all the provisions at my fingertips to make the most of your blessing of opportunities, the power of ideas and thankful reflections, all the sweet emotions from the myriad of connections with people who are intent on love and care, and then there are the things. Press upon me the difference, to love and care for the people, and only to use well and wisely the things, and to understand and cherish the difference.

Amen

Wednesday

O Lord,

I watched the snow that came lightly dusting the feathery arms of the evergreens on a wintry day. Such hushed beauty, quietly transforming the earth. Thank you for simple things. There is so much beauty to see all around us. Quiet this frantic pace of our fractured and frustrated world. Slow us into a gentle walk, Lord, that we may know its every beauty all the days of our lives.

Amen

Thursday

O Lord,

In my day after day struggle to be faithful, I keep remembering your call to be wise as serpents and innocent as doves. What a careful instruction to my reluctance to be interrupted. It is your invitation to unclench my fists and give my hands in wise kindness and kind understanding. Renew my excitement for the ongoing experiment of the work of love that builds the human family.

Amen

Friday

O Lord,

This is our day to celebrate love! How odd to identify only one day to regale the greatest thing in the world. Say it with a box of chocolates, a dozen roses, flattering cards to tease. But we will light up schoolrooms, neighborhoods, marriages, families and every relationship formed in terms of genuine affection. All of this with signs of warmth, appreciation and simple attraction we will be proud to say, "I love you!" But just for one day, one day to say we're trying to do what Our God did to create the heavens and the earth and everything in it.
Amen

Saturday

O Lord,

Friends are real treasures. Someone who shares the same interests and is interested in sharing it all…with me. The intricate thought you put into devising the intricate connection with a friend, it staggers the mind. It's electricity, it's wiring, it's contacts. Oh, the mind of God, and I see it in this gift. May I never presume, but never overlook an opportunity to be a friend. You make a believer of me with every new discovery. Everyone deserves the riches of a good friend.
Amen

Sunday

O Lord,

Today we will gather up again to say and sing out loud that the length of your love has outlasted the stubbornness of my sin. I am so glad that they taught me to come into the house of the Lord, the one place where I can shout it to the rooftops and be restored from within. I am so glad. Thank you, Lord.
Amen

WEEK 3

Monday
O Lord,
I really love our culture that encourages individuality and personal responsibility. We are so very practical. But one successful leader said that times like these require us to do more thinking and acting rather than praying. Lord, it grieves me that these two should be considered to be exclusive of each other. Is this becoming a cultural religion rather than a genuine faith? Lord have mercy. Make plain your distinction and your truth and lead us for that holy corrective if it is so.
Amen

Tuesday
O Lord,
I know your forgiveness is the heart of the gospel, and believe me, I am always consciously grateful, Lord. You give mercy for my weakness, a pathway straight to your heart, then your unconditional acceptance, so undeserved. Now I must live it, not a one off, but living a forgiving spirit for anyone? A one off is easy, but to have the spirit you have shown me, I cannot and do not do this on my own. Help me, for huge pride stands in my way.
Amen

Wednesday
O Lord,
"Delight yourself in the Lord!" If it feels this good getting used, for you to "use me," then keep on using me until you use me up! I am rejoicing knowing you can use me as imperfect as I am. "I stand amazed in the Presence...I will just keep on smilin!"
Amen

Thursday
O Lord,
I found a friend who is an immigrant to this land, her trips to visit her grandparents in their native land are spoken of with such fascination and reverence. She works so diligently and with gratitude that I am humbled and inspired to do better myself! How could we turn away these, your children, who are the promise of our future? Forgive us Lord, for we have sinned against brothers and sisters in need. Surely, "In God we trust."
Amen

Friday

Oh Lord,

We do not understand the Arabs. Their Middle East, a match thrown into a pool of gasoline, as a fruit seller burns himself to death. His whole life, as he said, was a life robbed of dignity. It is a breakdown in a social contract held with the governments and their people for generations. How have we been part of the unjust and unresponsive? I know you have cried out in the streets that we must learn to be civil, to be respectful, to love one another. Open our eyes as we struggle to open our hearts to others and show us how.

Amen

Saturday

O Lord,

Talking to someone who cares, who listens and who genuinely understands is something so unique, so beautiful, teaching me a forgotten truth, that I carry my burdens silently to my own peril. Sharing my concerns, pouring out my heart to a trusted one, my joy is multiplied, my sorrow divided. You, Lord, are teaching me again that it's okay to open up, because you do understand, and you are to be trusted. My God, my God, what a friend. Change comes at the speed of trust.

Amen

Sunday

Oh Lord,

"Give God the glory!" Lord, how do you do this? Athletes pointing to the sky when they make a touchdown? People surviving surgery successfully, saying "God answered my prayer?" Going to 11AM church? I remember that you are always on the side of the poor and downtrodden. I do not understand all of this. It is too broad for my small mind, but I just know, "God is great, God is good, let us thank him for our...daily blessings..." And I will always hold onto gratitude deep within and find worthy and understandable ways to communicate my thankfulness, always. Thank you today, Lord, for this day.

Amen

WEEK 4

Monday
O Lord,
"Are you preaching anywhere since retirement?" Asked so often and answered, "Yes! Everywhere, on the streets and in every chance encounter. I'm learning to encourage people with a positive and true word about their contribution and their worth." It is so refreshing and needed. Doing so comes easy, perhaps because I have felt the pain of words of sarcasm or discouragement, even the pain of silence when a good word would have been so easy. Lord, you have encouraged me so often, spoken to me just when needed... I stand amazed... Let me not be afraid to speak.
Amen

Tuesday
O Lord,
Keep me loyal, not blindly loyal just as a payoff for protection from those who will care for me, but loyal to the highest I know. Help me to show my loyalty to what matters by learning again the value, the treasure, the credibility, validity, sacredness of what matters most, my character, truly known perhaps only to you. Loyalty is on display all around, every day to me by those who share their plenty with those who have nothing, nothing of what we have.
Amen

Wednesday
O Lord,
I'm weary, weary of this old world. Sometimes it reduces me to tears, quietly, privately, but tears for how hard it gets sometimes. And my brothers and sisters, oh how weary they get trying to make their lives work. I heard my older friend crying, so tired. I watched the star athlete crying at the funeral. I saw the homeless girl weeping, "I can't talk, not now. Pray for me!" And she just cried, so hard, so weary. With your strength, you won't let me get weary in well doing, will you? Please hold onto me so I can keep going.
Amen

Thursday
O Lord,
Growing up has been such an adventure you created, great fun and still is. What a pleasure to learn to give up playground indulgences like pouting and pretending, bullying, and badgering. But the harder tasks like giving up grudges, a hateful spite, a hardening of the heart, and accepting the satisfying disciplines of getting up spry and joyfully eager to meet you in each new day, making needed adjustments without complaint, grinning and bearing it where needed and more. But when you taught me to forgive, to swallow my pride, to love my enemies, that seemed impossible and unfair, until you gave me that undeserved grace so lavishly. That sealed it for me, and I am humbly grateful, Lord.
Amen

Friday

O Lord,
You have called for a joyful life. "Rejoice! And again I say, Rejoice...be exceedingly glad!" Reasons? "For great is your reward... for his love endures for all generations...for so persecuted they the prophets..." For this wonder of being alive, alive today, and "full of the knowledge of the Lord, like the waters that cover the sea...!" Oh, I am! Yes! I am!
Amen

Saturday

O Lord,
You, Lord, are always the same. In this changing world, that is a miracle! The same for the pious and the prisoner, the populist and the priggish, the pauper and the proud, and they all have found you in their own experience, and you are always the same. Your greatness, your goodness, and all that we call gracious, that never changes. And all who call upon you, all, will find you, when we seek you with all our hearts. And so, I seek you.
Amen

Sunday

O Lord,
I got a recall notice in the mail about a defect in my car that relates to safety. Seems an emblem could come loose on impact, harming those within. Ha! Like my conscience bothering me, reminding me that the little twinge of pride that slips into my silent thoughts and makes me think I am slightly ahead of others, better than, more deserving, upon impact it can be deadly. Defect! Recall! Unsafe! Come to Christ again in childlike faith! Replacement parts are available. Please come in for repair. Jesus, I come.
Amen!

March

WEEK 1

Monday
O Lord,
Thank you for providing for this sweet man. He walked across a continent, bringing his family out of war and into promise and safety and opportunity. And we as a people, filled with your blessings and liberty, have had it to give, abundantly. His story resonates in the sacred halls of the church and in the often-tumultuous fields of our nation's politics, but mostly in the throbbing desires of my own heart. I watch from a distance as he raises his family and walks humbly with you. I am touched, humbled, inspired.
Amen

Tuesday
O Lord,
Partnerships are treasured, sacred throughout my life, your creation, and plan. I took vows to protect the one that you say would reflect to the world your own love for us all, unconditional, regardless of whether it is kept well on the other side, a promised covenant to protect, to cherish, to provide for, to love. Those vows I said before you and a host of angels who shook their halos and flapped their wings in agreement! You were right, and so were they. Strengthen me, for sometimes all these take work, and I'll show the world!
Amen

Wednesday
O Lord,
You said it is truth that will set us free. Never let me rise in such self-importance that I am too busy for the truth I may hear from others, or too strong to perceive a truth in something weak, or too hardened to receive new truth when it goes against my grain, or too self-assured to listen in a confrontation. Never let me slip from a determined love for the truth that sets me on a path to always find it wherever you may speak it to me.
Amen

Thursday
O Lord,
It's an imperfect world, and all of us have flaws. There is no none who has not made our share of mistakes. I've said it a hundred times while considering it a sufficient excuse for my own. How easily I watch the errors of others, especially those closest to me, yet I hear your words, "The one without sin may cast the first stone." I drop my stones. One by one I let each fall from my ready hands. And I stand alone before you, hungering for your generous mercy.
Amen

Friday

O Lord,

Busy, busy, rushing about… When do people like me pray? Can I speak to you on the run, or does it require the quieting down, the fervency, the regularity or constancy, the careful directness of an ancient connectivity? Is there some special ingredient, some right words, or may I count on the sincerity of my heart, an honest attitude wrapped in humility? These I can never forge from counterfeit. In awe and wonder I confess my simple, childlike trust, my great need, my love.
Amen

Saturday

O Lord,

Prayer is power, a gift you have given and that you have chosen us to use. Praying takes an act of pure faith and can never be counterfeited for any useless purpose. I admit when facing great concerns, I have too often thought only of myself, clinging to the things you have given me to share. I surrender to my fears and have pushed you aside, forgetting that you are "mighty to save." Reawaken my mind to your willingness to save me your way. Save me from my own shrinking ideas of being safe and secure. Set me free again, I pray.
Amen

Sunday

O Lord,

So many gifts you give us, and we cannot, do not thank you enough, unless perhaps by using them unselfishly. Use these prayers to encourage your children everywhere, the gathered and the scattered. Give us one more gift this morning, a spirit of unity. Let it come from your compassionate church, looking outward to all of the needs of people's hearts, and offering compassionate understanding and help. If we will do the work of love in all its many forms, we will show the world who you truly are.
Amen

WEEK 2

Monday

O Lord,
Many Christians are praying this season about drawing closer to you, but you are everywhere and closest to our needs. You call us to stop, take a look within, turn away from what has cheapened our riches of spirit and purity. Help me fight those strong appetites, those that tempt me, drag us all into brothels of pride, weakness, self-pity, and indulgence. I do want to discover the depths of grace, your undeserved help and passionate love. I want a fresh devotion to what is true and fair and just and freeing. I want your way!
Amen

Tuesday

O Lord,
You are the Lord of history. We say it in different ways. Some say "God is in control," while others say "God controls everything." We are trying to confess our faith that you are Lord of all, but our language betrays our inability to contain your wonder and greatness, our weak attempts to control you. While our language leaves us stumbling over concepts too small for an almighty, sovereign Lord, and renders us squabbling with each other, never let me imagine that your power bows to my feeble manipulations. "This is my Father's world. I rest me in the thought."
Amen

Wednesday

O Lord,
"O love that will not let me go..." I've sung those words a hundred times and felt the embrace of which they assure me. There are few things that grasp and hold me these days, and fewer still that I can grip and hold onto myself. I need this, I need that word, the assurance that you will not and cannot let me go. "... I rest my weary soul in Thee..."
Amen

Thursday

O Lord,
I am watching your new generation, and I like these folks! They have such devotion to each other, an open dedication to what is true, a strong determination to do right and to do well. I am stopped short, shaking my head in pride. They are so good, so refreshingly wholesome, so ready to care, to help, to think through, to be clear, to speak up. You have made them. They act like a church, so we must let them be our church and let them lead us.
Amen

Friday

O Lord,
I don't want to be like Mike. I want to be like Mack, like Liz, like Laura, like Harold, like Joe, like Anne, like Cheryl, like Ted, like Lisa, like Bill, like Elaine, like Tony, like Gail, like Jane, and so many others I see and know and cannot name. There are so many whom you have made with such gifts, such heart, such clear-eyed views; many who are willing to do what is necessary to be the difference. I don't want to be the one who just lives in the small world of self, but who lives with abundance that spills over like a mighty rolling water or a trickling stream, however is best to you, Lord.
Amen

Saturday

O Lord,
I am still watching your new generation. They drink coffee—good coffee, lots of coffee—and wine, don't shave, and don't have TV. They don't iron clothes, but they do iron out many wrinkles from my generation. They refuse to spend time on meaningless issues that don't amount to anything, but instead focus, and focus well, on clarity of what they deem to be meaningful for their times. And much of that is about their perception of what amounts to real spirituality today—energy, connection, truth, fun, fitness, and clarity. They are new and different, but did you bring them about or did I? I am seeking an answer in you, Lord, because I want to be relevant to their world if that's at all possible.
Amen

Sunday

O Lord,
Keeping up appearances is a deadly game. We can't have both a healthy spirit and a popular lifestyle. Lord, you call for honest admission of wrong to claim your offered fresh start, a confession, a repenting turning. These old words in our new age are just as good now as then for the same old condition. I want that renewal to a right spirit, to tend my heart, and I will only get there with your powerful, prevailing help. "Help thou mine unbelief."
Amen

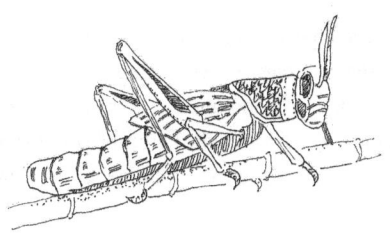

WEEK 3

Monday

O Lord,
Spring has sprung, and it's glorious, Lord. What glory, what subtle perfections! Schubert said he was finished with composing, and then he heard a clarinet. He went on to compose dozens more, more magnificent than before. Exactly! Winter has me down, I think, until I experience this bursting of springtime. I am ready for all you have for me. Bring it on!
Amen

Tuesday

O Lord,
Leaders are on full display at this hour in our history, as much with our issues as with any in history. We stand at a crossroads of pleasure and success, one that we have been careening toward forever as an affluent country. You, Lord, have blessed our nation, our decision making, yet now our way of life brings us to a logical conclusion: Is life all about me or we? Leaders are on display, those who have been anchored in your truth and those who have been hiding behind your truth. O God, this is another judgment day, and we find again, and we confess, that we are sinful.
Amen

Wednesday

O Lord,
You say, "Be still and know that I am God," and now I can feel it! For there is a stillness all over the land, a hush, an eerie calm. But I sense you are here. People are staying home. Our drivenness has settled down. Our activities we have come to expect, those entertainments we have thought we couldn't do without, all of that busyness is quiet. Is this the calm before some coming storm? In all this stillness, I do sense more of you and your presiding spirit, so refreshingly reassuring. O how I have needed that simple breath of life, and my heart is still and very thankful.
Amen

Thursday

O Lord,
These are uncertain times. The report is that experts said they were clear about being unclear. I will resist cheap answers that package everything up nicely but untrue. And I will reject a fawning acceptance of shrugging into a "no one can ever know" approach. I will live by faith in the lovingkindness of my God, my Savior, in the faithful record that we are never abandoned by an unchanging and eternal love, in your great faithfulness, your almighty power of purposeful will. I will hope on and do my very best.
Amen

Friday

O Lord,
I see genuine compassion cutting through the landscape of our greed, but oh how slowly, subtly, how meticulously deliberate, so barely noticeable at times. But it is there, almost as if it knows nothing of our timetable, our fabricated sense of urgency, our self-serving immediacy. And it cuts through with precision like a plow carving out the furrow for the seed that only you can produce. And we are the planters. Your seeds of change will take root, sprout upward, and grow. I want to be in that number, when your saints come marching in, quietly, steadily, plowing in with love and genuine compassion.
Amen

Saturday

O Lord,
We have lost our friend. She's gone, the breath of life snuffed out like a candle. She was reluctant to leave us, but eager to stop this suffering—some trade-off. She also left sadness, the deaths of her own, the disappointed dreams. Yet she knew the good years, the wonder of loves, the chance to be alive, her daughter, her son. We lost her, or did we just give her back? This first round was vibrant and full of meaning. What are your plans now?
Amen

Sunday

O Lord,
I have an invitation to speak, a singular moment to say exactly what is needed—again! That wonder, to speak a word of life… What shall I say? What must I say! What would others say? With all that is welling up inside me, for all that is stirring up around me, how do I cut through it all and choose what is essential, something that is so necessary as not to be missed? Only 15 minutes of attentive listening for the truth… What must be said? Lord, will you inspire and give me words? What will I say?
Amen

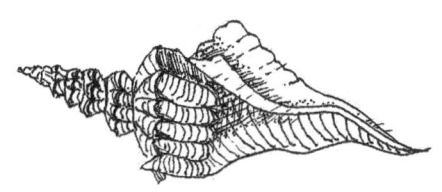

WEEK 4

Monday

O Lord,

I am singing, "Blue skies smilin' on me, nothing but blue skies do I see!" Silly songs? No, not of naivete' but of a diligent and resolute hope! "I lift mine eyes unto the hills, from whence cometh my help."

Amen

Tuesday

O Lord,

We spent the night in my wife's college guest quarters last week. It was lovely to awaken looking out over the Virginia hillsides while enjoying a warm comfortable bed and provisions. Not being a student there or having belonged, I had no one to thank. Today I awakened to a new day, and I knew whom to thank for this world. I am grateful, O Lord, that you have let me know you, adopting me to let me belong. Thank you.

Amen

Wednesday

O Lord,

As I dismantle my library for retirement, you are showing me an insight, of what a lifetime of treasures, thoughts, hopes, and interests I have collected. Now I will dispose some to friends, some to young followers, some to other readers, some to libraries and schools, some to trash. Some I will save to savor, reread, hold close. You too have treasures, senior saints, whose whole lives are libraries ready to be shared and you help hand these out. Let me help with such treasures and then read and read and read.

Amen

Thursday

O Lord,

Life can be so hard, but we have made it soft—the American Dream. Owning stuff, being in charge, reveling in freedoms and finances and personal protections: that's enough. It gets hard when I ask the hard questions again, trying to make things add up, to even the score, to make life fair, to prove faith works. Then it's what's inside me or not that makes it hard. Will you fill me again? I've sprung a leak.

Amen

Friday

O Lord,
People are so stressed out today that we all can turn such a mean side toward each other in a flash. It's a flash of temper we used to say, but it feels more like taking each other for granted, demanding our individuality over another's, pushing each other out of the way. What has happened to us? That's it: the us. The great gift you have given is for us to learn about belonging together, loving one another. That's the essential life-learning! Make us learn to care.
Amen

Saturday

O Lord,
One of your saints has called me, filled with hope at 99! In such isolation of age and mobility he wanted to enjoy contact, and hearing a voice helped. His best friend who died last week was breaking his heart until he thought that she would be hearing the voice of his own wife who died 10 years before, sharing their lives on the other side. "Isn't that something?" Oh, that is something! How that hope, defined only by my imagination, fills me and anchors me in hope! What a wonder you have created!
Amen

Sunday

O Lord,
Loving God with all my heart, the greatest commandment, sounds so hard, but it's really about how you live—respectfully. I will wander my neighborhood and behold your creation and your calling to springtime. I will plant flowers of praise and take care of myself, believing in my worth to you. I will think positive thoughts to demonstrate faith, expressing care for weaker and smaller ones as a sign of their value. I will not demand something for me but only to be something for you. To sacrifice a little becomes beautiful again. You are calling us to greater life, and I thank you.
Amen

April

WEEK 1

Monday

O Lord,
There are heroes all around me, those who have sacrificed so much to preserve life and the lives of many of us. They have what we need to raise up the next generation of heroes. These are not just smart; they are doggedly determined to do what is right, regardless the cost to themselves. You do require something of each of us: to think and to decide and to commit. Give us heroes who make a point to discern what is right and what is good and who are choosing to live it. I choose to be in that number, not a hero, just one who loves what is right, one of yours.
Amen

Tuesday

O Lord,
People on the go: that's what we are. We don't like to slow down or get quiet. That makes us uneasy, like it's wasted time. But sometimes I have to stall my motors to let your Spirit catch up with me. Then I'm not in charge. Is that where the ancient enemy has trapped me? I'm learning, Lord, but it's a slow process to turn this ship around. Be patient with me; don't give up on me. I want to be in that number, yours.
Amen

Wednesday

O Lord,
It's cooler in the mornings on the front porch than on the back porch. That simple element of sunlight makes all the difference, in degrees! "You who have made light shine in the darkness, you have made light shine in my heart." That has made all the difference, in degrees. I am humbly grateful for light, for warmth, for knowing the difference, and for a hunger for more.
Amen

Thursday

O Lord,
Walking out in your springtime, I was suddenly surprised by the stunning fragrance. It was a bloom, a flowering, stretching reach of intricate color and beauty. So unexpected, so subtle, surprising then arresting, captivating all my senses in its ambush… It was bursting with its own excitement, enjoying my dismay, inebriating me with its natural inspiration. A viburnum! I remembered gratefully the friend who gave it to us, the season that brought it to life, and the God who created it. Joy, joy, joy!
Amen

Friday

O Lord,

I have a nasty bruise, bigger than I've had for a long time. It came from a fall in the woods while helping a neighbor. I bounced up, protesting, "I'm okay! No problem!" Now I am surprised by the deep, huge, round purple thing and the soreness that came later, achy. I have watched it for weeks, often amused, then surprised, hurt, angered, and shared or sought a little attention. You have taught me something: There are hurts that come, some from falls, some from people who do not understand, some from the rigid edges of life around us, some from a long time before when misunderstood. Wait. Watch. Learn.. Pray. Forgive. Keep going, trusting.
Amen

Saturday

O Lord,

To my surprise, I have suddenly experienced a Sabbath. Quiet, calm, and it seemed the whole world was calm, hearing your commanding word, "Be still! I am your God. Experience this. Experience me, again!" I have seen and spoken to only a few closes people who are nurturing friends, and I moved around so little that it would have seemed unnatural, except that it felt like a healing of all the wounds of the world. "He restoreth my soul..."
Amen

Sunday

O Lord,

A young musician was very passionate about the music… Or was it the message? He was telling the stories of others who had heartaches, questions, struggles with life, and some who were suffering. I heard their stories as he jumped around passionately, and their stories came alive for me and I felt their prophetic value. Lord, you have prophets whom I do not recognize because they do not look and act like me. But when I listen, I hear your voice, your words, those answers, and your help comes through! Help me listen more.
Amen

WEEK 2

Monday

O Lord,

I heard a song today that lifted me right up to the portals of heaven, up from within the depths of my soul. Oh, that gift of music, those songs! Where do they come from? Deep in the hearts of these gifted musicians … and from your very heart! Oh, what a gift you give us, to treat our hearts with such tunes and such care, our emotions so gently and so rousingly, whatever is most needed. I am loved. We are loved so beautifully, so perfectly. Thank you, Lord.
Amen

Tuesday

O Lord,

I heard a singer-songwriter tell of having "friends in low places," ones who helped him when he had the blues. I get the blues, too, but I don't have friends who can listen, or whose similar injuries have been carefully put away. I have stayed away from those in low places, like these. I miss their stories of how they pulled through. Lord, you have prophets who weep about shame, who strip down to make a point, who stop eating to get someone's attention, who cry and scream about injustice, about robbing the poor, about suffering and loss, about life being unfair. I weep, too, and need those friends, so we can make it together.
Amen

Wednesday

O Lord,

You sent a friend who listened to me, my searching for words for my bundled feelings. He was patient as you are, not interrupting nor answering, letting me search around feverishly. It was such kindness in allowing me to flail around like a dog dropped into deep water and pawing feverishly. He didn't bail me out; he just stood on the shores of calm friendship, waiting until I found my way out. He gave me back my confidence, in me, in the value of the struggles, in you, Lord. Your gifts of life are so rich!
Amen

Thursday

O Lord,

Since I could not go to church this week, I was watering my newly sown grass, watching and hoping it would grow. Then I called my children, sharing my thoughts about my work and their work and futures. Suddenly I saw it! That's what church is, both a watering for growth and calling up our children. My, my, what a lesson! You said your Spirit was given to "lead us in all truth, to remind us of what you had said, to teach us." I accept this Spirit's lesson. What grade will I get today? But you came not to condemn (grade us) but to water us, to cause us to grow. You created church, far more than a temple worship, a congregation for watering and checking

up on each other, and that's essential. You gave the gift of faith and, as master gardener, you call us to keep nurturing faith.
Amen

Friday

O Lord,
It's almost Easter, and I struggle with the prospect of a miracle, so audacious and surprising a word. I try it on as a way of seeing, a way of living. I try to see it, hear it, understand it. It probes me; it questions me. This mystery is too wonderful for me, not a certain dogmatic knowledge. But the more I listen, the more I learn and the deeper the mystery. We are indeed fearfully and wonderfully made. O God, do not let me shrink your power into a size that I can understand.
Amen

Saturday

O Lord,
A friend called just to check on us. How very thoughtful, so considerate. He finished by saying, "I love you!" And it warmed my heart to hear those simple and familiar words. Of course, I knew it already, but how good to hear those words that he took the time to make this ordinary time such a rare and unforgettable time. Lord, make me so considerate and not afraid to say the words, "I love you." What a life-giving gift.
Amen

Sunday

O Lord,
I stand amid the others who stumbled toward the grave of Jesus, and I tremble. Weren't you there when they crucified my Lord? When they hung him on the tree? That shocking injustice, the kangaroo court, the criminals and cowards who nailed him as a criminal… That unimaginable cruelty left me blind and heartbroken, and yet now I see. I once was blind, but now I see How shall I then live? Within the living presence of Christ, alive and living among us, I am a changed man. Those others told the story: "That you might believe, and in believing, that you might have eternal life." I do, Lord, I do! Make me one of yours, now.
Amen

WEEK 3

Monday

O Lord,

The birds are having a heyday! Their happiness simply fills the air, drowning out any hint of darkened despair. Every inch of sky is filled with their music. What could they be singing about, so gloriously and proud proclaiming? I know! It is that a new day of hope has sprung forth from the wreckage of our world. O sing it! O sing loudly, unrestrained, and fill the skies and our tired old world with the news of Christ Jesus! It is the message we need today.
Amen

Tuesday

O Lord,

It was a black day in the history of this world, a dark and hopeless day, when the powers of all that we know is wrong and twisted had taken a fatal blow at all that we know is right and honest and pure, a time when we thought our God would stand up to all those dark forces that grabbed an upper hand to make a mockery of justice and all that is good. It was over, and we were left powerless. They had proven to be stronger than decency or civility, making excuses for their cruelty and having a free hand at dismantling what you, Lord, began at creation. Evil reigned for a day! You have had the last word, though. It is "free grace, free grace, sinner!"
Amen

Wednesday

O Lord,

How important to be right, we think. But your call is something qualitatively different. It is a call to be righteous, a word we seem to fear as it rubs up against the false quality of pride. To be right inevitably leads me to being correct, appropriate, all the time, and I can hardly resist being proud of it. To be righteous is to do what's right, and that's different. It can be costly, and if I have tilted toward pride, I will resist that with everything I am! Lord, I hear you calling me, all of your children, our nation and this world to righteousness, to do what is always right, regardless of the cost. I want to be that, so keep calling, urging, pulling me and all of us onward and up.
Amen

Thursday

O Lord,

By the people you bring into my path, you teach me something—old and new friends with whom I share so much. Many have been to church, were taught the essentials of who you are, Lord, and what life requires as made by your hands. The ones who had those lessons given early, before the world put them on the defense or taught them to always love number-one above all: they have a heart that is different, open, unafraid to care, to be vulnerable. It may not be strongly

on their shirt sleeve, but they have that love. Deep inside it's there, planted by you, Lord. And I see it right up front, and I can draw close.
Amen

Friday

O Lord,
There is something essential about talking with friends, something almost sacred. Yet, often words can come across as threatening, to be quickly brushed aside. I always long to talk heart to heart with a friend, to hear and to be heard, to understand and be understood. Lord, how does our fear raise up barriers between us, and for that matter, between ourselves and your Spirit of wonder and newness and opportunity? How much we miss. Keep trying, Lord. We are a stubborn people, a proud people, a fearful people. In your living presence I find peaceful confidence.
Amen

Saturday

O Lord,
I have been watching movies of the world at war, hundreds. We seem to glorify war with romance, intrigue, acts of courage, nations overcoming evil with unity and sacrifice. In spite of all that excitement and stupendous display of power, war remains a horrible blight on the soul of your creation and a shame on the souls of the people you created. We toy with the prospects again even now, murdering each other because we do not agree or cannot reason out our differences, giving rise to and permission to the violence that every single one of us are capable of. And though you provide a truth to set us free and a way to live above it, you warn us that there will always be wars and rumors of wars. Our pride can be so easily misused, misguided, mislaid. Have mercy on us. Help us surrender that ugly and death-dealing substance lurking in our hearts. Replace it with passion for your new community.
Amen

Sunday

O Lord,
In the quiet of the morning, I see your light tiptoeing back into this world of ours. Though it never left, you gave us rest, just like at creation. Now you give rest to our souls, our inner resources, our reflective powers, our thoughts and fears, our griefs and weariness. You have taught us to restore our inner reserves, to give it a rest, to be quiet within and without. O what a price we pay when we ignore this simple gift, this instruction, this original recipe. My heart is restless till it finds rest in you, Lord.
Amen

WEEK 4

Monday

O Lord,

The resurrection of Jesus is the gospel good news. The Lord who loved us is alive again, and even death couldn't stop him! It happened as attested to by those special ones closest to him. But the first words to them stand out to me: "Why do you look for the living among the dead?" What a commentary on our affections and our petty kinds of aspirations. We are proverbially "looking for love in all the wrong places." Guessing that means we are looking for the wrong idea of love, too? "O love, that will not let me go, I rest my weary soul in Thee; I give Thee back the life I owe, that in thine ocean depths its flow may richer, fuller be."
Amen

Tuesday

O Lord,

In a contact with a friend in quarantine, I needed the help of a nurse whom I found ready and eager though already much overextended. As we talked, he got me through, made the needed contact, expressed the love, gave the resources, shared his time and his life and his love. It all worked. As we closed off the call, he thanked me for treating him "like a partner in ministry." Of course, indeed he is. Aren't we all "in the ministry," we who have seen and believed the good news of the great healer, Jesus our Lord? Yes! We are partners, working in the greatest field of all of life. So glad you called, Lord!
Amen

Wednesday

O Lord,

Spring has brought a peaceful quietness, resting some and rattling others. I thank you for the call, your call, and the chance to rest the soul, the spirit, the mind, and the heart, and to bring them all together again. I have missed that and didn't know how separated, scattered these parts of me had become. It is a Sabbath rest, your ordained time to be restored by your hand. Thank you for these moments of furthering life, and forgive me for the sin of unknowing. How sweet is this peace, just to know it is possible and to be brought to the still waters again!
Amen

Thursday

O Lord,

I had rushed to the tomb of my own soul, but I did not find you there. You had gone on and left the message that you would meet me out in the countryside where they needed you and me. When I peered inside, I found the carefully folded linens of hurts I have inflicted on others, the wrongs I have accepted by my own cowardice, the anger that had built barriers between myself and others, and my part in injustices from thoughtlessness. I desperately need a word of

forgiveness, a cleansing hand of healing, a bridging path across the gulfs of my ungrace. O Lord, you know me, and I come to you. Where else would I go, as you alone have the word, the hand, the path to life?
Amen

Friday

O Lord,
A friend called her Bible teaching "Diggin' Deep." She dug up such deep truths, deep feelings, deep thoughts, deep yearnings in the hearts of those kids she taught, and deeper still the deep, deep love of Jesus. But it's hard to go there without a gentle and skilled guide, yet how important to the soul of believing in this fast generation. And we must go there if we are to keep this fragile faith ignited, burning, and making us real. Give us guides today, brave and worthy and genuine and deeply honest. I plead from my heart and soul to you, O Lord of the deep truths that save us.
Amen

Saturday

O Lord,
The country singer sang this hymn, thanking you, Lord, for unanswered prayer. He said he had asked for so many wrong things in life that would have sidelined his chance to live free and be faithful. I never thought of it that way because I have been so busy asking, begging, even demanding answers. I join the singer. I thank you for your perfect will. How can I say thanks for so much I have not deserved?
Amen

Sunday

O Lord,
Easter has come and gone for us, a tradition, a celebration, one Sunday's reflection. Now our lives move on. For those who met you in the flesh it was never just gone, the experience never left them, and they were never the same. Touched by such astounding power, they were left to make sense of what happened, what they had seen and experienced, and to live in the light of your claims and your claim on their lives. What a wonder to behold and to live for, especially in a skeptical world that must have thought they were crazy. Don't let this experience ever leave me. I will never be the same.
Amen

May

WEEK 1

Monday

O Lord,

We're saved by grace. My friend said he found that grace was the little surprises interwoven into his life by the people who treated him with kindnesses. I remember being taught that every life is like a blank canvas, and we all hold the brushes that make the art in each other's lives. Are we the bearers of your grace to other people, as the body of Christ? Let me be an artist, one whose colorful pallet reflects all the rainbow of your kindnesses.

Amen

Tuesday

O Lord,

Laughter … a good belly-laugh with friends, chuckling, shaking with delight, cackling and shrieking with head-shaking, side-splitting guffaws and gasping for breath…What a happy gift you made, and we need it so much! Yes, it is as Solomon said, a merry heart is good medicine. And you are indeed the Great Physician, a healer of our souls, oh blessed Lord and Savior!

Amen

Wednesday

O Lord,

I am a believer, not the kind who needs to wave a banner in the face of opposing forces, but the kind who holds on tight like a drowning sailor in the storm. I am clinging to the broken masts of the ship. This does set me apart from many of my friends, people I admire, whose energy sets them apart. Their diligence and positive spirit are admirable and call up my greatest admiration. They believe in something, even with greater strength and sturdier unmovable conviction than I. Which do you prefer: the desperate clingers or the diligent overcomers? Or do we all have a place at the table?

Amen

Thursday

O Lord,

You have called for believing as the stuff of life, the overcoming power to live the abundance of life. I do and I feel that confident hope within that is indeed life-giving. So much is settled within as I come to faith, believing. And I know the discoveries of science and medicine and other solutions in life are also included in your grasp. They are part of your creation, too, all of this you have made available to us and given us the mind to search out and use it all to live. But dying comes to us all, the change that no one can avoid. "Accept!" said the deacon to me. But you said "Believe!" And this, too, is transforming, masterful. My Lord and my Master, I cry out like Thomas!

Amen

Friday

O Lord,

Yummy and delicious! I thank you Lord for leafy green lettuce, for crunchy red tomatoes, for snappy green beans, for bright crisp carrots and all swirled in pungent oils and strong vinegar. The purple and green spring onions made me cry, but those were happy tears as we laughed and munched them together. The fresh and tasty delights were right out of the garden, growing in your rich and fragrant earth. What a partnership you have shared with me! I am delighted. I hope you are delighted too, Lord.
Amen

Saturday

O Lord,

I am a pilgrim, just a wayfaring stranger, a wanderer in your world and sometimes feeling lost in a wilderness of noisy demands. Once you led by a cloud in the day, then by fires in the night. I yearn for such clear assurances, not mere talk of your leadership. Those desperate people found their way because you led them. Lead me again, Lord. Make your way clear before me again. I do not want to awaken one day to find I was only going through the motions of following you. I wait, and I am watching with fresh eyes, and I am pressing on. Lead me, Lord.
Amen

Sunday

O Lord,

People everywhere come on this your day for that refresher course. Remembering Easter's promise, we cannot ignore that true worship is about giving: Yours is done; now ours is all that is lacking. O today, tell me again that what I bring to you—offerings, time, attention, patience, reflections, needs, hopes, understandings—is about demonstrating how much faith I really operate with, about really believing with all my heart! I want to bring real gifts in wholeheartedness again. Help me, Lord, to get out of the shallows into the depths of your power and love just one more time.
Amen

WEEK 2

Monday

O Lord,

I see children everywhere, and sometimes I stop to watch. One today was with her mother, shopping for essentials. Mom was busily intent on her business, as was the child. But the child's business was to enjoy, to express herself, to drink it all in while walking with her mother. She was skipping, waving her arms, fluffing her hair, talking and singing to herself, occasionally breaking into a short run, then skipping again. Oh such delight and freedom and trust! Childhood is so beautiful. Let me be childlike in my heart.

Amen

Tuesday

O Lord,

I work and live among other adults. They seem so distracted, so busy, intent on going somewhere. Though many like to wave and speak, seldom do we share anything about our lives, what is on our hearts, what occupies our thoughts, where we are going—if anywhere at all. Many seem tired, worn down, disturbed, in a hurry for what I don't know. Are we all running after something or running from something? Are many running after you, Lord? Will time run out for most of us and we'll say, "Ah, I made it … to the finish line"? And what will you say to us, each one of us?

Amen

Wednesday

O Lord,

Thinking about the greatest commandment, to love you, God, devotedly, heart, soul, mind, and strength: That takes so much reverence for life and a seriousness that I cannot seem to enjoy consistently. Sometimes it makes me dull, and I am afraid of being dull. It makes me have wanderlust! I just enjoy everything you have created, immensely, and some of it is hilarious. Can I be hilarious and still be holy? In fact, I am enjoying talking with you, Lord—openly, freely, and a bit joyfully, I admit.

Amen

Thursday

O Lord,

I know a truth from one of your great scientists, one I cling to with a tentative but hopeful belief. It stirs me on days when I reach down deeply for something to cling to. It is this: "If you love something enough, it will give up its secrets to you." I do love many things, and so many of your people, especially. Sometimes I know I don't love persistently enough as a determined scientist might, or selflessly enough as a consistent servant of your love should, but it is there in me. I ask that you love me enough to make be better at it, because I do want to love as you love.

Amen

Friday

O Lord,
I see a buttercup, so tiny and peeking through the grasses. Do you see it? Of course, you do! After all the other attention-commanding blazes of spring glory, there is still room for one more, this tiny delight. You see. You made it. You planned for it. You delight me. It captures my eye, my breath, and my imagination. How wonderful are your thoughts! The tiniest ones matter.
Amen

Saturday

O Lord,
Sabbath is coming, a day of rest observed at creation. Whew! I know that was exhausting, seven exhilarating days of making meaningful and purposefully interconnected living things emerge, set in motion, to thrive and feed on each other in a wholesome interdependency. And just look around on this spring day: it's magnificent! Silently colorful, brilliantly alive… Where was all this greenery a month ago that has burst forth for me? It lay dormant in seed form in your rich and verdant earth, hiding along with all the sleeping life below surface … the wiggling, the squirming, the shivering, the snoring, the life appearing lifeless but ready for your call! Today I wait; tomorrow is for resting, surrounded by your glory.! And I hear you calling!
Amen

Sunday

O Lord,
I love the quiet of a Sabbath day. In the stillness I can sense you, O Lord, near and real, strong and gentle, approachable, peacefully present and watching over your creation. I can sense again that you are God. I can sense what holiness feels like. It is better than good; it is that longed-for perfection. You are holy, and you care for me!
Amen

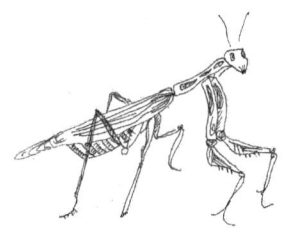

WEEK 3

Monday
O Lord,
The simple joys of a walk around the neighborhood, to hear the birds, feel the breezes, listen to the earth and the sounds of your own soul. Both are alive, moving, going somewhere. Always there is some silent moving, some quiet reaching ahead, some momentary standing still, some dying, though most of it is unseen, undetected, and never rises to the senses. The movement of life holding within the move of your Spirit, both of us—you and me, partners, companions, co-creators in life. And you included me. Oh, the greatness of God!
Amen

Tuesday
O Lord,
Oh, this faith is good! What a sure hope, startling me back in the darkest times. Lord, keep me trusting, believing … in the family of your beloved, the washing of my sins, the resurrection to new life, and the clear guiding of your Spirit. What a real and sure hope! I am real and full of hope.
Amen

Wednesday
O Lord,
I saw the tiny pansy you planted in the crevasse in the wall, showing me that you can make life happen in spite of the walls we build. Such a surprise to discover your subtle and stunningly beautiful little reminders in the most unexpected places! Your power of life is greater, more persistent than all the disappointments I may face. I am persuaded to no longer fear the walls, for nothing can stop your persistence.
Amen

Thursday
O Lord,
I hear more and more easy talk of heaven, even a claim on it as the expected promise, an assumed reward for all. Familiar assumptions sound like the whole substance of faith. There's little mention of God the giver, no reference to a relationship with or a faith in the one who calls us to follow and walk that lonesome road. Others say, "I hope I make it," as if it is the earnings of doing it all correctly. Talk of heaven gives an enviable relief, a confidence, a heady and light-hearted acceptance. I am glad to shed the guilt of a frightening punishment from an angry God, but I have thought our priority was to be on loving and seeking the giver rather than the gift.
Amen

Friday

O Lord,

The Psalms tell me that continual praise and thanks to you, Lord, are rightfully due to you, God of the universe, creator of heaven and earth and every living thing. There is another message: that being thankful puts things right, puts me right. That is the key to a devotional life, to daily mass, to the treasured quiet time. Yes! It is the food of a healthy soul, the medicine of a sin-sick soul, the joy of a happy person who knows the Lord as heavenly Father. I know that in my head; help me get it more in my heart. Then help me get past my exhaustion and love the discipline this requires.
Amen

Saturday

O Lord,

We surely talk a lot about love these days. "Show 'em some love!" we say… Hugs, warmth, cheers, happy celebrations of who we are, who they are, and what they do. Make noise, press the flesh, give a little in support, share what you have, give a little, give a lot! Those moments mean a lot. Real love lasts longer—lasts for a life, lasts beyond—and real love is something that never becomes anything else. Jesus calmly, thoughtful showed us that unchanging quality. And it got better, stronger, richer, more meaningful under fire and still never changed, never gave an inch. Thank you, Lord. We needed that.
Amen

Sunday

O Lord,

What is your idea of church, and is it changing for you as it is for us? What are its essentials: baptism, or kneeling, or offerings, or bowing, or gathering? Young folks say they can do it without the pomp and circumstance, the grouping and the creeds. The old folks say it only happens when we gather, when we pray, when we sing praises. I know there can be healthy ones and sick ones, obviously, and some surely are quick to point fingers and call names of each other. What about peace? Could that be the essential ingredient, something only you can give and give in abundance? When we have it, when it's real and deep, it makes us real. And there is the difference. "Our hearts are restless till they find their rest in you."
Amen

WEEK 4

Monday
O Lord,
It's Monday, and we start it all again. For some people it will be a fresh start, so needed. For others it will be Blue Monday. They unwound the knots of life a bit too fast, too hard over the weekend. They don't have the umph to start it all again, to try to keep up the efforts one more time. But it is only just a continuing of who we are, what we do, and why we do it. We need to ask the "why" question first. I know why: "God is love, and those who live in love know God, for God is love." Thank you, Lord, for your actively busy and sustaining love, even when I least deserve it.
Amen

Tuesday
O Lord,
Our greed is despicable, depending on which side you are standing. Chasing after and grabbing all you can get for yourself… Got to have all you can get! How simply calming and liberating to know you are had by something, possessed by someone, like you, Lord. And what a world of difference to know the difference.
Amen

Wednesday
O Lord,
I am taking hot, fresh cookies to the post office today. May that bring them joy as I point them to the source of my joy. May my life of faith bring encouragement and offer appreciation for them as they serve us all in their tiresome roles. You care about them. Help me not to forget them.
Amen

Thursday
O Lord,
There is so much pain and sadness that it has pervaded the darkened wintry season for many. It is hurtful when I see it lingering in the hearts of friends. Have we mischaracterized faith as only a worrisome concern with no power? Or maybe to have faith is seen as only a call to a "get going" demand? Help me reshape the faith that I live and proclaim it as an active trust in an active and present God whose power can pervade and transform life and all lives. Help me be authentic.
Amen

Friday

O Lord,

I am reading the many offers of items for sale to "strengthen your faith," making it sound as if something needs shoring up, something hard to hold onto. Yes, it may be a struggle during times of challenge that test my soul, but what about the mustard seed-size faith? I am very weak, I admit, weak of spirit. But I do love you Lord, fiercely, and that one thing is greater than faith and hope, you say. My faith is honest, if not flag-waving powerful. I rest in your promise to use the weak things so that the glory seen and gained will be all yours.
Amen

Saturday

O Lord,

I have friends who are first-class skeptics, not deniers, but staying safely within the realm of "what if." Many of your children are like that. Instead of church, they grew up and continue in lives focused on staying energetically busy and productive. They're very good stewards of their time. Social media has taken over and satisfies the connection instinct. My friends hike, bike, paint, plant, exercise, walk dogs, do big family groupings and games, include others, and chat a lot on the sidewalks. It is a lot like church was once, people sharing their lives, their values, their thoughts, and their mutual respect, time, and truths that make a difference. These do a good job of answering the hunger for high touch. Will church regain them and reclaim these values?
Amen

Sunday

O Lord,

Have you been watching these peonies this season? Sorry, silly question, but they are exploding all over our yard and neighborhood! No one else could create such dazzling beauty—such mysterious shapes, colors, contents—and deliver them in such grand fashion. They are worshipping their creator, singing, lifting holy hands upward, then bowing in reverential honor. Honestly, I see how we could be more like them in worship and hope that we could be as lovely and bring you such pleasure. We do have all the makings, thankfully!
Amen

WEEK 5

Monday

O Lord,

Taxes, titles, passports, licenses: all this clarification of my identity, all these documents certify that I am who I say I am. But whom do you claim me to be? Prayers, promises, pledges, commitments, certificates, certifications, degrees: all these that I have offered to you when I so needed assurances in my uncertainties, answers in my questions, assistance in my need, an anchor in the storm, an anvil to forge out my identity. "All my trophies at last I lay down… I will cling to the old rugged cross, and exchange it someday for a crown."
Amen

Tuesday

O Lord,

I took an early morning walk and ran into one of your truly celebrated servants, one who has made a consequential difference in our community, and we talked. I haven't seen her in months, but we talked as old friends do, picking up right where we left off, our hearts deeply engaged in the love we have lived to express and exert. It was a touch so many of us have been lacking, a touch of the hem of your garment, a healing and restoring touch, touching the body of Christ and being made whole and well by the simplest of reassurances. It was only a moment's exchange, but it cast a flickering light into the darkness—just a touch, a potential we all need and all of yours have it to give!
Amen

Wednesday

O Lord,

Bluetail skanks are everywhere, peeping out from behind the rocks, risking a moment in the sun, staring at me, wondering if I am safe. Neighbors are leaning on and over the balconies, waving curiously, interested in my comings and goings, questioning my projects, offering to help. The bluebirds have a nest, but the hawks are threatening and chasing them. The colors of life are so lovely; the interwoven lives are your handiwork, your plans, your purposes for us all. I love to learn about your thoughts as I enjoy this project, a quiet and carefully laid-out drama of life. Can I help?
Amen

Thursday

O Lord,

You have a servant in my neighborhood who loves your artistry and tends your garden of creation. I learn from her; we all do. She loves what you have done. She loves nature because in it she sees plans and purposes, gets directions, learns reverence, watches love unfold, and follows suit. She learns from you as she plants gardens, tends flowers, pinching them when they are

finished. And she talks to them as she watches birds, feeding, housing, and watering them. I think she knows you very well. I think she has seen your face.
Amen

Friday

O Lord,
My friend has lost his wife, or truly has given her back to you. They had so many years together, and it is hard to give up one whom you have loved for a lifetime. We are not prepared after a long companionship, sharing our lives together. Though we say we are not afraid, still we are shaken down to the core. Life is so uncertain, and our days are not guaranteed. That seems so unfair, so mean and unnecessarily cold and heartless. I cannot offer the standard phrases we all have heard, not out of my sadness for my friend. I can offer only that which we both believe: that you are greater than all our sorrow and good beyond all of our understanding, though it hurts so much.
Amen

Saturday

O Lord,
In an interview a pro athlete said: "We need sports now more than ever. It helps to keep us active, focused, well, just alive! I don't mean any disrespect, but for most of us, reality is hard, and sports helps lift us up above it all." He had been a rough guy, a loud and demanding young player, but now is a man who helps his community. He has been rewarded, lifted above it all, lifted to see it all with fresh eyes of respect and concern. He sees people working through their struggles with determination. He is interested in them and sees value in their lives and now shares his benefits. I like his spirit, and I feel your pleasure in him, too. Oh Lord, send us more like him.
Amen

Sunday

O Lord,
A friend who came to the sanctuary for a community weekday assignment commented: "This is a lovely space, so light, so peaceful. I don't ever come inside, so thank you for sharing this with me." Then I realized it seems so routine for me, and I take it for granted. It is your gift to us, allowing us to be calm here, to reach up, to shout out, to weep, or to bow down and collect our senses, our perspective again. I sit in silence here now, and the quiet is healing and more than calming. There is a presence here, and I know that we are not alone.
Amen

June

WEEK 1

Monday

O Lord,
My buddy likes golf better than all the sports and keeps it up even as he grows older. He describes it like this: "You aren't out to beat the other players. You are competing with the course. Sometimes it beats you up when you can't get it together, and sometimes it is real forgiving." We need those lessons about how life is just like that. You aren't out to beat us or favor us if you are pleased with us. Life's paths are made, and we play the course. But you are always teaching us how to be our best and enjoy every minute, winning or just slogging through a rough patch. And you encourage us as your pride and joy.
Amen

Tuesday

O Lord,
It's the aimless people, the plain ones among us who get in trouble, because they get in the way of the focused, the well-directed ones. We push them, shove them aside, curse them for getting in our way. Then we hate them, fear them until we think we have to deal with them, and we do it with justified force. We allow it. They got in our way. Your way is to talk with them, value them, direct them, heal them, love them while confronting their wrongs and offering forgiveness. They respond to that. When will we learn to do it your way?
Amen

Wednesday

O Lord,
I experienced a miracle today, and they call it surgery, just a small one—always small if it happens to someone else. The surgeon takes a tendon, pulls it around another joint now worn beyond usefulness, and it's new again. Surely many people were crippled through earlier times without this simple healing procedure available. The repair is a miracle you shared with us, as with those you loved and touched and healed. What more will you share with us as we prove better stewards? Oh, help us to slow down and listen and care. And thank you, thank you, Lord.
Amen

Thursday

O Lord,
People are crying, crowding the streets and trying to make us listen. They say they can't find a step-up beyond their station in life, that we have denied them the same chances we all have had. Am I a privileged one, one with more than enough? Have I failed to listen to their pain, their fear, their frustration? Does the fact that I don't know what to say mean that I have prejudged their condition, or not paid attention, or not believed it, or have not cared? What do you require of me? Who are they? Who am I? Why don't we know each other?
Amen

Friday

O Lord,

It seems like Christian people, the Christian life, and the church are focused on taking care of sick people—comforting, praying for, assuring, supplying food. This is beautiful grace, but have we become afraid of pain and just feeling bad. We don't want anyone to feel bad! But I learn so much in my sicknesses, like how I depend on you, or how I have ignored and neglected my relationship with the God of my strength. I may get the blues, then curse the world and all my troubles, then I awaken to all the riches of my life and feel foolish. My love for you, Lord, is reignited. I need that humility, a gift gently given. Yet I never take another's pain lightly or for granted. Make us compassionate and unafraid to touch the lepers, but also wiser in your gracious plans.
Amen

Saturday

O Lord,

A caterpillar has eaten my redbud tree, and it seemed so unfair. I had brought the tree from Georgia, nurtured it lovingly, proudly. Had I invaded the caterpillar's territory unnecessarily and unfairly? It stung me when I touched it, crawling its way toward the sky defiantly, colorfully, ceaselessly. Who's in charge here? Who has dibs on the land, the trees, the growth? Am I the intruder? Do only the strong survive? Am I right in asserting my strength here, now? You are teaching me about making room for all, despite our many differences.
Amen

Sunday

O Lord,

It is another Sabbath for resting and renewing. I can hear the machines running, cleaning, mowing, scrubbing, painting, building, transporting. Above it all I hear the birds, the music, the wind, the babies crying, then noiseless stillness. We have redefined rest: it is whatever we most want. It's our free time, and we have forgotten that giving you the time, you are able to restore our souls. Lord, are you weary with us? Call to us one more time and we might hear and come, for the spirit is eagerly willing. But the flesh reaches for the path of least resistance, for the pleasure zone, clinging to the comforts of our culture, seeking to suit itself. It is weak, so weak, weak indeed.
Amen

WEEK 2

Monday

O Lord,
I filled out my reminder list today: prayer and take out the trash. These two, or is that one—one and the same? As I stand before you this morning with arms outstretched and hands open, I am vulnerable, open, radically open to you, Lord. I realize that I need to take out the trash; a painful unloading is a necessary part of being able to pray. I know that honesty is what you require for me to be able to hear and understand anything from you. Help me, for I want to do what I know you are asking of me: to really pray.
Amen

Tuesday

O Lord,
How do we do sadness? We have everything and more, don't we, and sadness doesn't seem to belong in our realm. We have worked every angle to eliminate the specter of sadness and have almost achieved it, as if it is the American dream, freedom from want and sadness. But it is slipping beyond our reach and eluding our grasp, for we cannot ignore the hurt in our land, the land of the free and home of the brave. This sadness is deep in my bones, for these are my countrymen crying out from the soles of their feet and the depths of their hearts. Lord, you have always heard my own cries, for a lifetime. So I, too, must listen and bear this sadness with them.
Amen

Wednesday

O Lord,
Heaven is shouting the wonders of you, Lord, and every living thing shows your perfect craftsmanship. How could anyone doubt you or ignore your ways? It's just knowing how to live in sync—what's yours, what's mine, what to grab and shape, what to leave alone. Where are the lines of trust? Where do I take over as you planned? Where is it right to say, "Just accept things as they are"? Ah, now I see! Day after day you are speaking to us, and night after night the insights still come pouring in. In every word spoken in every nation you can be heard when our hearts are right with you. Yes, it's getting clearer now.
Amen

Thursday

O Lord,
While it is still and quiet, remind me how to seek the kingdom, things the way you like it, how to work for your will "on earth as it is in heaven." First things first: set the pace for me before things gather speed and I am caught up in my routines where I seek things in heaven to be as they are on earth.
Amen

Friday

O Lord,

I heard Mary singing, "Don't laugh at me." And her song was this: "Because in God's eyes we're all the same." And the room became really quiet, and then they all sang along. This is what she was known to always be saying: "If you're gonna sing the music, you gotta live the music." And the world has been changing since she sang. And this is what the prophets said, and they said it was from you, and the world has been changing, slowly.
Amen

Saturday

O Lord,

How often have we been singing this line, "Something happening here, what it is ain't exactly clear"? Some of us could be lifted out of a reeling sense of despair and a helpless feeling of futility if we would begin, for a change, to think of other people and what we might do for them. Lord, come and heal some lives in these days. Heal them of self-pity and bitterness by helping them to reach out with generosity to people with greater needs than their own and to causes in which they can lose themselves and where they may find themselves fresh, free, and joyful again as you meant for their lives to be.
Amen

Sunday

O Lord,

We know more than people did in ancient days. We know you are a God of love and grace, forgiving and merciful, holy and reaching toward us in our need to regain a holiness for us as well. Our real wealth is in you, not in what we own and accumulate. Still in our worldly wealth is a natural and needed way to grow our spirits by sharing what we have to alleviate the sufferings of other people. Help us break away from our fear of giving to discover your giving. Help us to embrace being the blessing to each other, the will of God.
Amen

WEEK 3

Monday

O Lord,
Another day begins and I pass by the busy beginnings of wide-eyed neighbors. They gather flowers, pull weeds, walk their dogs, drive around to go to the mountain for a hike. They plan to bake a cobbler, pick up a new cat, meet friends on the golf course, let workmen in for repairs, or just sit quietly with the morning news… And life begins again. You created a beautiful family and taught us the key ingredient: to love one another, actively, openly, and warmly; celebrating the differences and the beauty of each one, sharing the space, then bowing to remember the covenant promise—the call to follow, the order of light and dark, the show-stopping wonder—that you are God. And then a baby is born somewhere!
Amen

Tuesday

O Lord,
It's early out, and fresh, and still wet with dew. As I walk, I can feel the prayers of people swirling around. They are reaching out to you for your hand, your voice, your quiet and simple assurance of your watchful and attentive eyes. Your voice is clear and strong. But that hand, it has a deep wound, pierced with an angry spike. And the pain it brings is the shame I feel that angry people wanted your voice to be silenced, your touch to be withdrawn, your eyes to look away, for love to just stop it! But that incessant love never stops. And I am so humbled, awed, grateful, and so undeserving. Love persists.
Amen

Wednesday

O Lord,
Friendships are such treasures, simple connections, sharing our lives and laughter and our living experiences. But simple friendships, what a calming and affirming pleasure to sit for a minute and share a moment of life, a story, a chuckle, one of those head-shaking ironies found along the way. Just look what you created, Lord. And then you said you no longer call us the religiously proper term "servants," but "friends," because you are sharing with us everything—everything, from wisdom, to heaven's plans, to the riches of this earth, and all the details in between. What a friend we have in Jesus, all our wrongs and their heartbreaking consequences, losses, misunderstandings to bear… My friend.
Amen

Thursday

O Lord,
Have mercy! You must be exhausted with us. You gave us Jesus to know the truth, to find our way and to live as you intended. I bow before you, my heart yielding to your love. Yet all people

do not honor you. Some set military might over your almightiness, human thought against your all-knowing, selfish schemes above your concern for all people. Some hear only a cold, stony silence from what they think is an unfeeling cosmos. Let the rulers of this earth see a glimpse of your grace and see that yours is the ultimate victory over every enemy, that yours is the power that satisfies every heart, heals every wound, supplies every need. In you is the answer to every question we have.
Amen

Friday

O Lord,
I heard Whitney Houston singing that song again, a pledge to always love you, and I choked up. The passion behind her naked promise of devotion, the stirring in my own heart to love like that, the raw emotion it brings from her and from within me… But my broken heart comes from the pain of knowing she is dead—dead from the drug of our success culture that stripped her of a sense of simply being another person of honest human value, a child of God, with one life to live before you. So overwhelming was her pain, she had to resort to hiding the terrors in her own heart and her own family with drugs—drugs that we have made so easily accessible to her, we handed to her, so that she could keep singing for us. Now there is no more song, and I weep.
Amen

Saturday

O Lord,
Now comes the sunshine! The warmth on my face after the evening chill is a welcome friend, its companionship so friendly, its brilliance illuminating everything around me, its warmth on my shoulders like a friendly arm to draw me close. And then it smiles on me, surrounding me with a reassurance that it's here to stay: I'm here, and I'm here for you. "What are people that Thou art mindful of them? You made us a little lower than the angels."
Amen

Sunday

O Lord,
This is to be a quiet day, the one where some divine hand weaves back into our souls the one thread that gives it all color, light, and meaning—the thread of grace, woven all throughout the whole tapestry; the day, the mood, the feelings, the memories, the reflections, the yearnings, the sadnesses, the griefs, the joys. In this day you will restore my soul, taking the raveled edges to bind them up again, tightening what is tattered, protecting what is worn, rethreading what is torn. Take me, Lord. Take all of me. Retread my weary soul, for I need the colors of grace, the face of my God.
Amen

WEEK 4

Monday
O Lord,
I want to thank you for prayer. I have so much inside of me, pouring forth into nameless, faceless speech, and no one else could possibly understand or bear it all. But you, Lord, you take it all—all my sins and griefs to bear. I open my heart, so grateful that you can and will take it all as it overflows over the edges of my soul, spilling onto the ground below. Your lovingkindness is better than life as my life overflows.
Amen

Tuesday
O Lord,
Another good and delightful servant of yours is a gardener, and I love her Saturday display of greens, so rich and colorful, so promising for good health. "Come and help me weed," she says. "I love weeding with friends. We just talk a lot. Then when we stop, I look up and see how much we have done. It helps me see my whole garden better, the wide sweep of what we have planted. Come help us!" And I am thinking of my soul, how I need good and careful friends who know my soul like she knows the land, and who can help with my weeding, so badly needed. As Robert Frost said, "The woods are lovely, dark and deep, and I have miles to go before I sleep."
Amen

Wednesday
O Lord,
Early morning people are happy people, eager to see and hear what has already begun at your masterfully careful hands. Two ladies at coffee, an outfitted runner stopping for a drink, my mechanic, a writer from D.C.... all openly interested and curious about my curiosity. "What are you carrying? That something you're reading?" And the writer said the world is glutted with people trying to be spiritually interesting, but hungry for someone who is authentic, someone who dares to know and live the authentic gospel, one they have heard but never yet seen. O Lord, "I would be true..."
Amen

Thursday
O Lord,
We rode on the Blue Ridge Parkway yesterday, so lush and green, and all was so inviting that we were naturally drawn in deeper and deeper, joyfully. We continued to ride until the rain came, pouring, surprising, soaking us with its refreshment. It had warned us with the darkest of clouds, but we had doubted and dared it! It came anyway. This is the growing stuff of life that comes for "the just and unjust alike," that blesses the good and fair as well as the mean and selfish the same. Yours is a fairness that we have not yet learned, nor have we conceded that it is equally deserved.

We do not yet know your economy. We still live by our rules, but we long to find your "more excellent way." Maybe someday, please.
Amen

Friday

O Lord,
Heal, sinner! How many times I have used that expression jokingly, but not now. I have seen one who has, and I am excited beyond words. What a changed man! I spent time helping him through a crisis a few years ago, and now I see him holding strong, a good job, self-respect, full of esteem and plenty proud. He had lost so much but counts it all for the best now. He's healed up! I cannot tell you how wide was his smile, and mine to match. I know he has pleased you as you filled him with hope and the courage to change, and I am bursting with happiness. One down and millions to go!
Amen

Saturday

O Lord,
It's quiet outside, a welcome stillness that is so rare. "Quiet as a mouse," Mama would say. No sound but a few waking birds and my breathing … the world is waking. It wakes to your presence filling the silence, a magnificent presence of passion and love that stirs every living creation to life, a love that enfolds us in the power of life and wraps us in an unshakeable promise of more life. This day is the new beginning of life all over again. Fill me again with that magnificent obsession like yours.
Amen

Sunday

O Lord,
Sabbath is for rest, something we are so reluctant to do in these days. O Lord, how I would like to stop the rat race, the treadmill I am on and give to you, to present to you a day of rest from my labors … a day in which you really can be praised as I reflect on your acts of love and power; a day in which you could have control, you could take over and do what you want to do, yearn to do in my heart and my life, and in the hearts of us all, and in the heart of our nation. We are on a fast track and cannot or will not stop. God save us! "Jerusalem, Jerusalem, how I wanted to take you under my wings, but you would not." And I weep with you.
Amen

July

WEEK 1

Monday

O Lord,

The hardest thing to hear is my friend saying, "I don't have time for worship." But we made time for physical exercise, believing it made us feel good and kept us healthy. And I ask, can the body exist without a healthy spirit? Can we afford to choose one over the other? Can the spirit be at its best without a healthy body? Like asking which blade of the scissors is the most important? Lord, call us to you and sharpen each blade!

Amen

Tuesday

O Lord,

My pharmacist is part of your people, for I see her with the family at church in worship. I enjoy the contact, and going in the shop, "I miss your high school helper." Yes, she is with her family today. "And where is your assistant? Gone home early?" Yes, we gave him half a day. We talk meds, ailments, usage, new products, children, and weather and wish each other well. It's like that when you belong as friends, and local sharing is part of the visit, more than just a product pick-up. Belonging is a sweet and thoroughly indescribable simple pleasure of being connected. You have made a family out of strangers. "And this is how we know we have eternal life, because we love our brothers."

Amen

Wednesday

O Lord,

I heard the priest reflecting, "What we are doing here is making room for prophets." You have always spoken loudly when we strayed and ignored your guidance, and those prophets have gotten in our faces, not to terrify us, but to urge us and warn us of serious consequences, as a loving parent warns her children. Scolding only comes after we do it anyway. We need your voice, your guides, your care. How much room is enough? Have we made enough room for the ones who are crying out to us now, enough room to keep your voice, your prophets, your loving care close to us? What does a prophet look like?

Amen

Thursday

O Lord,

I was helping and learning with one of your senior saints. Really, they all are walking, living libraries. They have been through so many years of striving, falling, picking themselves up, getting back at it again. Their stories are the stuff that makes us believers and makes us try again, too. I walked with him and slightly touched his back, patting mostly to let him know I was

there, close behind. I heard him mutter as he walked away, "That pat on the back feels good." Help me not to take such little things for granted.
Amen

Friday

O Lord,

Most folks keep up and stay engaged by reading their newspaper, so I left out early to get mine. Early is such a nice and unique time of day, and it belongs to the focused and the determined. I like being among them; they have much to say about how the day will turn out, each day being a gift they seem to appreciate and receive so willingly and gladly. I sat and watched a few busily getting their early starts, and one had a limp. He seemed almost more determined and prouder than most, headed into the store to start the day. And many of us have a limp—most, I believe—and we are most determined, because we believe you are determined.
Amen

Saturday

O Lord,

I hear a lot of the short answers, and I bet you do, too. "It's fine." "I'm good." "We're done." "No, uh-uh." Short answers just don't settle the big questions. Our issues of life are not that easy. Are these then the brush-off, a signal that we don't want to be bothered? I know I whine ofttimes, but please don't stop bothering me, Lord. I need your wisdom. "Thy Word is a lamp unto my feet and a light unto my path."
Amen

Sunday

O Lord,

I hunger for you today, not the culture, not all the frills that attract and tantalize me and hold me usually. No, I hunger for you. Could I handle it if you spoke to me, dealt with me, sidled up next to me for a while? I need to talk over a few things, things I do not understand. I want to quickly say I trust you, but a word from you would help. We have whittled your time down to an hour, but we could try all day again, just to drain the stagnant pond, then listen again, intently. You deserve that, all of my attention.
Amen

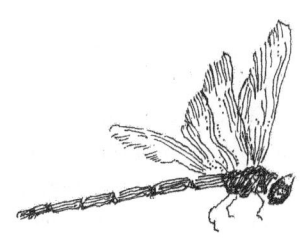

WEEK 2

Monday
O Lord,
"May all our alleluias, both spoken and heard, be heartfelt songs of praise to thee, dear Lord, and not just empty words." I pray these words again from the Gatlin Brothers' Band.
Amen

Tuesday
O Lord,
As I cleaned out a basement long unattended, I heard you speaking. Clearing out unused boxes and empty flowerpots, wiping away mold and mildew, sweeping cobwebs and dying flowers, rounding up postdated magazines once thought to hold valuable words, saving aside a few forgotten books, throwing out the trash… I thought how much has accumulated unused in my sentimental but reluctant heart. Make me a vital servant for good, Lord, for endless cleanup is so much useless work, draining away those good desires to be true. "I would be true, for there are those who trust me."
Amen

Wednesday
O Lord,
My friend has lost his mind, but he is happy. He doesn't know where he is or where he is going, but he is gentle and kind and willing. He doesn't remember who I am, but he knows we are friends, and he is always glad to see me. He has walked closely, obediently with you for many years, but now he cannot serve. He cannot pull his thoughts together to speak a word. His life, though diminished in what we say counts, still thunders out a call for justice, righteousness, and mercy for the broken ones—the essentials! The picture is changing of what is valuable now. O how you loved him before and surely love him now, as I do.
Amen

Thursday
O Lord,
I asked her what she thought and she answered, "Whatever." She hasn't been led to believe how valuable her thoughts are and doesn't know we truly value what she might believe is best. So many people force their opinions on us, on everyone, that some never have been encouraged to believe in their ability to arrive at those valuable conclusions from their experiences in life. All your people are not leaders, but all have valuable points to add. It's the value of each one, their own experiences. These things make us all clearer about what is at the heart of all our life together. It's about valuing each other as you do. Show us how.
Amen

Friday

O Lord,
"Don't worry! Be happy!" It has become a mantra for our age, a right not to be taken lightly or taken from us. We are told to go to our happy place, as if it is a state of mind where everything is gonna be alright. "Are you alright?" It's all that matters, this moment of having it all together, being safe, being secure, being happy. It's a place where everyone smiles, laughs, and has someone and they are embracing lovingly, kissing. We're happy. It's a destination, one that we did all this work for. It is a perpetual weekend, a Saturday, a day off, pretty alluring. And I am made to want it and told to believe I deserve it. "Man looks on the outward appearance, but God looks on the heart."
Amen

Saturday

O Lord,
Your best gift, my wife of years, has just had her arm cast removed after six hard weeks. How thankful we both are! Lord, you provide healings and give lessons in the process. I have learned again how much she has continuously done to make this house a home, without a whimper, and I have been exhausted in the reminders, taking up the slack. I have learned to do and keep on doing, in season and out, and not complain—the hardest part of all. I have learned again what it means to love, her love becoming more evident, and my love to be pulling my share. It's a working proposition! "Beloved, let us not love in word, but in actions... Beloved, let us love one another, for love is of God."
Amen

Sunday

O Lord,
Your day is a day for me to be still and know, or experience you, and I want that, but I have things to do. My busy life has daily requirements that mount up when I don't keep up, and recreation is a necessity to take when I have opportunity. My friend said, "I know whom I will vote for. So why keep on listening to more and more news?" Yet all the world is changing, daily, and life's demands are unending. How life-giving it is to dwell on the knowledge and to experience it, that you, Lord, are the unchanging center of this spinning and constantly changing world. Hold me to embrace the Sabbath. Even you needed one at creation!
Amen

WEEK 3

Monday

O Lord,

It is a powerful truth to be loved by you, O Lord. It is more powerful even to know we have been gifted to love as you have: patient, kind, not self-seeking, but listening, caring, not counting all the wrongs but celebrating the best in each one, and so much more. We all grow up and discover this gift. Then we have to choose to live by it or die by it! It thrills me to hear the promise that all that is incomplete will one day be fulfilled, completed, and we will see you and know you face to face. That's the greatest thing I have ever heard or imagined! O help me love and anticipate love's fulfillment every day of my life!

Amen

Tuesday

O Lord,

Everyone has a story. So how do you keep up with us all? An old military man, a wealthy inheritor managing family wealth, a child of a dysfunctional family, a son kicked out of his home for his uncooperative spirit, a widow just getting by, a young lawyer who has done everything right and is successful at everything he touches, a young stroke victim, a dingbat whose beauty opens every door, a bright community worker full of hope, a struggling food person trying to make a cafe work: We all are affected by the personalities of our parents and early relationships, some damaged, some bright, some tentatively plotting each uneasy step. And you are there, within each life, each heart, passionately loving, nudging, attempting to guide, giving us freedom. Lord, how do you keep up? Your mercy and kindness are an anchor, a rich resource, a gift. "O glorious victory that overcomes the world!"

Amen

Wednesday

O Lord,

That mockingbird is a voice thief, and he is right outside my window, shrilling his song or the ones he has heard from all the others around him! What a trumpeter he is, so loudly proclaiming his message for everyone. They say that when he gets alone, he regains his own voice and it is good. How am I be like him, showing off what I have heard from others, hiding my own heart from them, from myself, and from you? How do I fail you so often when you gift me with my own strengths and value? Make me more like your image as it was in the beginning.

Amen

Thursday

O Lord,

A summer rain is falling, gentle, cleansing all the earth, washing off my tension and struggles, refreshing my soul, quieting my mind. It is a lovely gift of yours, Lord, so unexpected but so needed. "O how he loves you and me. O how he loves you and me. He gave his life. What more could he give?"

Amen

Friday

O Lord,

You promised to be present with us. How could I forget? We are only three months down the road from Easter, but how could I fail to thank you? We sang, "Joyful, joyful we adore thee," but now I cry out for you to restore my rejoicing, because life is tough, and the way of your kingdom is not always easy. I feel the pain of disappointments, the humiliation of my failings, the isolation of ethical commitments, the anguish of hopes unrealized. Help me to know much more the joy of your salvation, that my stony heart can sing again, because the giver of joy is here—right here with me.

Amen

Saturday

O Lord,

Thoughtful is the term we use about someone who takes the time to show a kindness, a patient helpfulness to me when I am in need. Their act often overcomes my thoughtlessness and my impatience. Impatience has caused much pain, rashly making demands on others to settle some rush to judgement or an unwillingness to take the time necessary to bring about a more thoughtful response. They are exhibiting great restraint, real selflessness, the very substance of what I most need. But we are in such a hurry, acting as if we can little afford to delay some action I think must be taken right now. That is my selfishness. Lord, give me grace where I don't deserve it. Your thoughtfulness can make me a peacemaker, too.

Amen

Sunday

O Lord,

Help me to worship today. Lead me in paths of righteousness for your name's sake, or for regaining a grasp on and broadcasting your greatness. I know what worship is: It is to awaken my conscience by your holiness, to feast my mind on your truth, to cleanse my thoughts with your wonder, to pry open my heart to your love, and to devote myself wholeheartedly to please you. I will be quieted by your love. Show me your way, and show me the path.

Amen

WEEK 4

Monday

O Lord,
As I heard the sadness of a friend who has seemed to struggle all her life and never seemed to get ahead, I prayed and asked for your special favor. She is so dear and so badly in need. You answered! And I think you spoke to her through me and through my faith. "Never let the past disappointments rob you of God's future appointments." I didn't think of that on my own, and I surely need that word to myself. I will seek out and trust a bit more in your word to us today. After all, you spoke the whole world into existence.
Amen

Tuesday

O Lord,
I love the pouring rain, the unexpected raining down from the dark clouds that threatened then surprised and suddenly appeared from unseen corners of the heavens—almost as if to wash the earth's trouble away, or at least to cleanse the pallet. These have inspired our songs of "Showers of Blessings," thanking you for the "mercy drops round us are falling, but for the showers we plead." Times such as these call for the gushing waters of evidence of your powerful, cleansing goodness. Please! Sometimes only the fount of every blessing can wash away our bent to hurt each other.
Amen

Wednesday

O Lord,
Little words of wisdom have been passed along to me and built character slowly but surely. Words from someone who really loves me always stick like glue and cannot be erased. "Pretty is as pretty does," my mother said with a twinkle, and it took! By your word you created the heavens and the earth. By her words she created a person with a soul, a conscience, with an insatiable desire to please her because she loved me. Indeed, your love is creating more than our eyes can see—now!
Amen

Thursday

O Lord,
I saw a "lost and found" basket at the door, full to the brim, and hadn't seen one anywhere in the expected places in quite a while. The name fails. All of it is lost. None is with its owner. And although it has been found by someone else and turned in to some place of keeping, it all remains lost until it is claimed again by its owner… lost, lost to circulation, lost to the usefulness it once had for its owner, lost to the safekeeping of its usual place, lost to its purpose. Most things

lost never seem to find their way back to the hands of their owners, but are just left behind, forgotten. As I reflect, it makes me sad to apply it to our own lives… so many… lost.
Amen

Friday

O Lord,
Death has struck and robbed one of her life, your gift that you so generously give to each of us. We all have been robbed of her life, your child, one of your precious ones whom you loved. Our only hope is in your word to us that because you live, we, too, shall live. You will have the final word, and that will always give us hope. We shall live!
Amen

Saturday

O Lord,
It seems so right to have Saturday preceding Sunday, a day to busy around and take care of all the cares, then to drop the load of worries at the end of an exhausting day of expending all my energies on my life. I am happily looking to collapsing into a big easy chair, thankfully awaiting a focus on your life, a restful day on Sunday, and having my soul refreshed from heaven's perspective, your essential reminder. "I will look unto the hills, whence cometh my help." But the temptation is strong to ignore my inward life. Hold me tight. I made a promise, and I live in the awe and wonder of your promise.
Amen

Sunday

O Lord,
In the quietness of this day, I pledge my whole life again to you. You are my strength and my shield against the pain of misunderstanding, against abuses of this age, against illness and suffering and pain, against uncertainty, against my own failures and weaknesses. You are my light and my salvation. You are my help and my hope. In you and you alone do I find the strength to carry on. I am rejoicing in the reunion you have saved me for, even the promise of life eternal, for it is your face that will be my reward. Nothing I have done can qualify me for the promise of this gift, but I am rejoicing in this covenant of life.
Amen

WEEK 5

Monday

O Lord,
I have a friend who struggles to live, an admired friend, brilliant mind, courageous heart, gentle giant. He reads Job and says the best gift friends give is not the expected advice, heroic stories, or faith slogans. The best is friends who tell him in silence, "I am with you and I trust God is, too." Help him, Lord, and help me to put less trust in my words and more truth in my living expressions of love. I want to love as you have loved me because he deserves this and more.
Amen

Tuesday

O Lord,
Your good servant, my friend, said she had read the scriptures saying, "We shall be fruitful in our old age," and she is working at that, enjoying that, delighted with opportunities she sees to do exactly that.! "I don't need it! I am cared for. And I see all these wonderful young people who are aiming so high, fearlessly, that I want to help." The joyful anticipation in her eyes was contagious. Lord, you planted that seed and so many like it, and in your word, she found the defining challenge—a simple discovery, a suggestion, a word, your word. There is a famine in the land for your word. Lord, give us more and more desire to read and rediscover.
Amen

Wednesday

O Lord,
"The earth is the Lord's." A man here who loves bluebirds has provided more than 30 houses for this radiant little bird. But your bluebirds have had a bad year with abandonment issues. They built nests then left them without a mate or a family, or had eggs and abandoned them, or had baby birds and left them to die without care or food. Abandonment, left alone without your provisions so generously planned… The answer seems that there are no insects, no bugs to eat, not allowing these birds to fulfill their care of their little ones. We have heard a familiar cry: "Father, why have you forsaken me?" But what are we doing to your creation? Our greed is stripping your creation of your finest gifts, as we ignore the plans of life you give. "… And they know not what they do."
Amen

Thursday

O Lord,
I held the door for a tiny lady struggling to walk, a simple kindness. As she stood at the door, she struggled to catch her breath and gripped the railing to steady herself. Then she volunteered her story to me as I waited… so much difficulty, physical pain but plugging right along. What hardships some live with. Forgive me when I whine. I have my health; the world is mine. Give

me more opportunities to help and to encourage these whose life is a struggle. A little means so much to some unexpectedly.
Amen

Friday

O Lord,
A beautiful attitude is no small matter and can light up a room, an unmistakable gratitude to you, Lord. I never met a soul who didn't like to be thanked when thanks were due. Surely you, too, smile when we realize that all we have ultimately comes not at your discretionary grace, but from free grace. Even suffering Job said, "Stop and consider the wondrous works of God." We do need to, I need to, ponder the mystery and the majesty of your creation, an earth that is bounding with all we need for food and cover; all the provisions and the sights, the delights, the wonders; all that keeps us exploring and learning and harnessing; all just as you planned for our wonder and gratitude. I want the attitude that displays my joy, all the time.
Amen

Saturday

O Lord,
Through the years I have observed friends whose hearts are purer than mine, who put me to shame, who live carefully and fruitfully for themselves, whose care for their own is incredibly good, dependable, and faithful. Yet I see their "religion on hold" ... good people, skeptic perhaps, but whose ethics are blameless. How is it possible to be such good people and yet practice no religion, no worship and thank you, no study of scripture or search for truth, no component of commitment to service, no consistent sacrifice or giving beyond the sporadic, occasional do-good act? They have found a certain peace with themselves that still eludes me. I can learn, we all can, from each other and yet from you.
Amen

Sunday

O Lord,
There are still some heroes yet! "Some don't preach sermons; they become one, bloody but unbowed, on a mission bigger than personal ambition." Sometimes time stands still to take note. Let the saints celebrate, and let the angels rejoice that one did stand down the evils of this world. They still meet Jesus and take him across the bridges that unite us. Lord, help me celebrate today but recommit to carry on tomorrow. Let the nation say, "Surely goodness and mercy shall follow me all my days, and I shall dwell in the house of the Lord forever." Lord, you do remember us.
Amen

August

WEEK 1

Monday
O Lord,
Faith is your gift, and what a treasure of relation and confident love you give us. As I hear many people speak of having faith, it seems like a quality someone gained and rose to the challenge to display in the face of difficulty. I long to hear them say, "I have faith … in God," because of your greatness and goodness. Faith is not a character element of mine but an experience of trusting humility, a childlikeness, a blessing received in light of your character of unearned grace, such as an innocent child embodies because of a strong and good parent. "It is by grace through faith…" If faith is my achievement, I would be working now to grasp it. But faith has grasped my heart as you have grasped my life. I bow my face, weeping in gratitude, Lord.
Amen

Tuesday
O Lord,
Do you attend funerals with us? I guess not. We are doing better, calling them "a celebration of life," and much better than the past, "dirges." I dread them and drag my feet when preparing for them. "This is my last one," I always complain, because they are painful … sad to be with those families, recreating memories, reflecting on what is past and who has been lost. We look inside the box, dressed so nicely, touch a lifeless and cold hand, or hold up a decorative box full of incendiary remains, pictures all around. It's all we have left, we say. All the while they are dancing somewhere with you, somewhere. I won't go again, unless we sing, and we can sing them to heaven.
Amen

Wednesday
O Lord,
Troubles are our biggest conversations. They are common to us all, though so different to us all. An illness surprises, a disappointment hurts, some loss trips up our forward motion, some truth proves not so, a trusted friend turns away, or the money runs out. Are you the author of our hurts? Is their purpose here all for our ultimate good? What a marvel it would be if it's true that "God is in control," and not only are solutions as your work in our lives, but by your loving hands around the clay of our lives, you are shaping each of us with these broken places. "Though he slay me, yet will I trust him."
Amen

Thursday
O Lord,
I have many friends who reluctantly tell of abusive parents. Horrors! What would it be like, fearful, ashamed, not aware that this is not normal, so limiting to a child's personality develop-

ment; so confining, twisting of their world view, and then such a driving force to their children's future planning and choices? Yet my friends—good, sweet, very fine people, and ethically impeccable—they have done so well, made such good lives. Yet I feel their pain that will barely show its effects in some limitation, something that robs me of their full commitment to a friendship. Abuse! We are all robbed by it.
Amen

Friday

O Lord,
I sense it is an important time for a change. Is this your nudging, or am I merely weary in well doing? It is an usual kind of blahs for a Christian. We get bored and seek adventure, or we feel guilt for not having more of a clear view of purpose. This stirring comes often as I look over my life, my use of time, my sense of values, my world. Where is the significance, the direction, the deeper level of meaning? Others struggle, one is dying, another is waiting for time to catch up to die, another needs a job, another has a lifeless marriage, another goes through the motions and the monotony of indulgence, and another lost a lifetime spouse. I care so deeply for them, but I cannot change things for them. Or can I? Can we together? I feel it is your nudging and your stirring within me.
Amen

Saturday

O Lord,
I stopped briefly down the road from my house. I'd forgotten something in the back of the car. Suddenly the whirring of tiny wings startled me as I looked up to see a defiant hummingbird just feet from my face, staring me down.! She buzzed away but had made her point. I was in her territory, just a short distance from her nest. I was an unwelcome threat to her little brood. It seemed familiar. I have seen that look, that angry look before, and not known I was in someone's sacred space, threatened by my ignorant presence. How often we threaten each other, or misunderstand each other, or even harm each other unknowingly. Calm my spirit that I may be more the bridge than the troubled water. There is more than enough hurt in our world.
Amen

Sunday

O Lord,
You rested after creation's wonder and delight, and you ordained that we should follow suit. The create-and-rest cycle is holy! Bless the Lord, O my soul ... and all, all, everything—all the moving parts, all the stagnant resources, every thought, every strand of effort and energy, each little unused and waiting portion, heart, head, and hands—everything that is within me. Bless my God who gives me such a guiding hand, who blesses me with a heart to feel, a mind to think and reflect, and a soul to experience and express myself, such as I am. Oh, the wonder of it all, that God loves me, blesses and redeems me where I fail. I will bless you, Lord, with all of my heart.
Amen

WEEK 2

Monday

O Lord,

Your hydrangeas are stunning! How long did it take you to make them and to design them so they would change colors? Ours burst out a stunning mint green, then become snowball white, and slowly morph into a final periwinkle blue, dazzling in the bright sunlight ... hundreds of tiny blooms on a single stalk, all perfectly arranged to make the large flower we think of as a single bloom. What artistry, what synergy, what mastery to fashion this beauty! Are we also as dazzling in our colorful changes in life, our shaping together, our pleasure to you? I pray that we are, though unbeknownst to us yet pleasing to you.
Amen

Tuesday

O Lord,

The large and lovely deer surprised me today, standing silently as if a sentinel over your deep forests, then stealthily slipping into the trees and vanishing ... its brown and mottled coat, its tiny hooves concealing and covering any trace of its perfect form. Beautiful creatures of yours, and you have so many of them. Their diversity staggers the mind when I think of their cohabitation. I know you take pleasure in every creature of your making. And then there is us, each one different, but made in your own image, differing in that way from these creatures. "What are we that you are mindful of us? You made us a little less than the angels."
Amen

Wednesday

O Lord,

I asked one of your faithful servants at 98 what he would do with another good, strong year. He answered: "I'd try to deal with what really matters. One is money, what we do with it and what it does with us. We can do so many great things with it, but if you accumulate it, it can ruin you. Money has made fools of some of my finest friends." And I remembered what you said, Lord: "It's the love of money that is the root of all evil." It's not foolishness, but it's evil as you see it. God help us!
Amen

Thursday

O Lord,

I overheard your conversation with an old and tired veteran of the Second World War, one of the few, the brave, still left. As he closed his eyes, he said to you: "I think a lot about killing people. I don't feel guilty, just that our civilization isn't doing any better now. Now we hate everybody, and they hate us. Somewhere back behind there, there has got to be a prayer. That's all you can

do. There had better be a prayer." So, I am singing my prayer to you now: "Lord, listen to your children praying. Lord, send your spirit in this place. Send us power, send us love, send us grace."
Amen

Friday

O Lord,
I love the mountains. I love the rolling hills. I love the flowers and all the daffodils. I love the fireside when all the lights are low. And I hear your words to me, "Except you enter as a little child, you shall not enter the kingdom of God." Gladly, simply, I come. Struggling to be in charge, I come anyway. Fearful of letting go, I come. Uncertain of a future where you alone are leading, I still come. I am coming, slowly, reluctantly sometimes, but humbly I step out of my little boat into your stormy sea, with you. I come.
Amen

Saturday

O Lord,
The beans are all in! It was a cry of pride from my church group. They had been given an abundant crop this year, made full to overflowing by plenty of rain and sunshine, then so much dedicated attention by your people—willing hands and hearts, joyful spirits; happy people, giving their time and dedicating their attention. It is more than beans. Their joy is a partnership with a good, loving heavenly Father, the Creator of beans and bearer of glad tidings. "I bring you glad tidings of great joy … unto you is born a Savior!" Then they gave the beans all away! The beans are gone, but their joy is still here with them. They are your church.
Amen

Sunday

O Lord,
I hear the songs of faith today, or is it the hosts of angels? I hear the words of life today, or is it creation's calling? I hear the happy welcome to worship, or is it the call to come home? I hear the prayers of your people, or is it the Spirit's giving words for groanings too deep for words? I hear the silences of the hearts of those gathered, or is it the quietness of your peace you give, the comfort of the Spirit giving credibility to the truths you spoke to us? I feel the warmth of my friends and neighbors surrounding me, or is it the presence of the Lord? I worship you this day, O Lord.
Amen

WEEK 3

Monday
O Lord,
There is so much coming at us for change like never before. So much is too much. Fear and mistrust are gripping us and whipping us into a frenzy, "full of sound and fury, signifying nothing." And you said some of the strangest things: about loving your enemy, blessing those who curse you, doing good to those who hate you, praying for those who despitefully use you and persecute you, "that you may be children of your heavenly Father." How can this possibly work, rolling over and letting an adversary, an enemy get the upper hand? This does not fit with the ethic of this day. How can you, why would you turn us into weaklings? What will the enemy think of us? On the other hand, what will you think of us if we don't?
Amen

Tuesday
O Lord,
I walked down to the small river and was surprised as I stood beside a swollen creek, the trickle that is now a mighty river from the rains, full of rushing water, tossing the rocks and tumbling the debris from the mountainsides. Its raw power is beautiful in its strength, pushing through everything that dares to stand in its way. And I hear your prophets proclaiming, often angry, often desperate, sometimes pleading, telling of your cry to let justice roll down like this—like a mighty river, pushing, cleansing, carving out a new way, impatient to bring a fresh spirit of freedom now for all your people. And I know these familiar words, and I feel the familiar resistance. I cannot do it alone, but I must do something. Bring the rushing waters, Lord.
Amen

Wednesday
O Lord,
There are fresh vegetables from the garden, and our neighbors are sharing. We picked them and brought them home to eat. Bright green and yellow, their shapes and color alone make them wonderfully artistic, but the taste of them is nourishing and delicious—more of your perfect handiwork! You give food to all the creatures you created. And I read, "I have never seen God's children go hungry." … Body, soul, and spirit: Let all the creation and its creatures praise you!
Amen

Thursday
O Lord,
Sitting here watching the pouring rain, summer showers come so quickly without warning. I love it when you open up the heavens and refresh the earth. I can feel my spirits calming as everything has to simply stop. I am reminded how your blessings come rushing down in torrents sometimes and then in trickles at other times, but always coming. I am reassured, knowing you

care for all living things with such remarkable fairness. I want to be more like that. You tirelessly "send the rain upon the just and unjust alike."
Amen

Friday

O Lord,
The Psalmist asked, "Why do the heathen rage?" I wonder the same, though I think I know the answer. Every day there is a "do or die" proposition. They have not heard the long dimension of your love that changes all the dynamics of our fears, or the record of your faithfulness that fills the minds and hearts of people who have heard your story, or your pledge to care through the joys and heartaches, the lifetimes of each of us because we matter, each one. The rage is about making up for all those injustices of life by getting back at someone or defying the odds that there would ever be another disappointment. But there will always "be wars and rumors of wars," and there will always be your promises.
Amen

Saturday

O Lord,
Yours is a love that will not let me go. I do not now, nor have I always understood it or appreciated it. When asked, I say I am doing better than I deserve, and I mean it! I know that I try my hardest to do all I know most of the time, but I fail. I fall short, I get lazy, and I whine about how hard it is sometimes, how unfair life can be, and how I wish I could go off somewhere and just enjoy myself. But your love will not let me go. You have not given up on me, so I cannot, will not, give up on doing my best. Because your love will not let me go, and I am so thankful.
Amen

Sunday

O Lord,
Out of this noisy world and the constant strife of wagging tongues, I come to this quiet place to worship and turn to you. You are never far from any one of us, but by our own insensitivity we do keep you distant. Today is a new day, full of opportunity. Help me to be receptive that my heart and soul will welcome you.
Amen

WEEK 4

Monday

O Lord,

I listened and watched in reverence to a man you have loved and shaped and used in many remarkable ways. He told me, "Growing up in the country, all my friends were black. Whenever my folks traveled, I stayed with Uncle Bill and Aunt Hildy, my other family, a black family. When I was in trouble, I ran to their house. Then I remember when we set 'em loose. Was a great day because it was right." Help me to know what is right when no one else does it, and what is wrong even if everyone else does it. And help me to do what is right, whatever it costs me. What we do echoes through the generations.

Amen

Tuesday

O Lord,

These days can grow awfully dark, visiting the dying, digging up dead flowers, jumping off dead car batteries, and sharing in dying churches. Lord, the work of care seems a heavy burden at times, one that only can be handled with your hands on the swords and plowshares with me. Help me see this important work as planting seeds for tomorrow in the same grounds that produced these other good gifts. The soils are made richer by the turning under of these plantings that have shared their souls, spent their time, and blossomed in their day. And their blooms have been so lovely in their time, tending their world. Help us, help me, help us all as we work, partnering with you, our Creator and Sustainer.

Amen

Wednesday

O Lord,

How can I say thanks? I am wondering ... When a friend says thanks, it is appreciated, sweet, but it's just words. So often I rush about and forget, but I realize how grateful I have been all day, enjoying all your good and perfect gifts and knowing full well where they have come from. Really, it does me a world of good just to stop and list the things you have done for us all, things so undeserved. Yet, as I do, I become more aware of the gifting, and many more gifts—the perfection, the grace of life, the perfect timing, the remarkable artistry. Then I realize that I don't know how I can ever say thanks, well enough or appropriately enough, or enough at all. When I offer thanks from my heart, my whole life becomes larger. How wonderful! What a gift it is to give thanks!

Amen

Thursday

My friend called to say he almost died! I am shocked! So close to home and I didn't notice. I have taken our friendship for granted, sharing time but not the deepest values of my heart, taking

that for granted, too. How much I take for granted in my life! I don't know what I would do without him. Missing his friendship would be bitter, knowing I never told him about what I take for granted that he never had the benefit of having. Waken me, Lord. Wake up my lazy life to the treasured friends and the greatest gifts I have that I have taken for granted and the chance to share the very best.
Amen

Friday

O Lord,
What's the difference between faith and respect? An honest question seeking an honest answer … I am seeing some people of faith whose living example is pure debauchery, embarrassing and humiliating before the public eye. I am finding many people of genuine respect whose lives are more consistently free of wrong, who spend serious time making wise judgements and expressing sound decisions so as to be respectful of life and of others. Friends of faith often seem most concerned about who gets to go to heaven, while these friends undefined by faith but more by respect think those end times are more respectfully left up to you, Lord. Does faith include respect? Does respect generate faith? Is the proof in the pudding? I am asking.
Amen

Saturday

O Lord,
I see Kevin, Barbara, Allen … Real people with names and whose lives are a big part of what I depend on to make my life run smoothly. They call me by my name, too, and we greet each other heartily, enjoying the chance contact. When I know their names, I take them seriously … Real people with real lives that matter and who experience challenges daily; face dilemmas often; have families, hurts, and happiness; spend time building community networks; and make choices constantly that build up or tear down their own lives, and unmistakably mine too. We are part of the fabric of life, a tapestry of meaning, the cloth of creation. And you are the God of all of us. What an amazing God, our Creator and Redeemer!
Amen

Sunday

O Lord,
I awakened to the sounds of the wind and the birds, and then I heard a far-off whistle of the morning train. Your world and our world … What a contrast. You gave us everything, entrusted it all to us to enjoy, to use wisely, and to be nurtured by it, while we care for all things. So many people do their share of caring by what they use; others just use it all and expect the resource to be unending—at least in their lifetime. Only one day is reserved for you, one day to bring the two worlds together, to help us believe and say again, "on earth as it is in heaven." Will we see it? Will I? Can we say it loudly enough to mean it and spread the word about the help available? I will "be still and know that you are God!"
Amen

www.ingramcontent.com/pod-product-compliance
Lightning Source LLC
Chambersburg PA
CBHW071006160426
43193CB00012B/1935